A DIARY OF PRAYER

A DIARY OF
PRAYER

COMPILED BY

ELIZABETH GOUDGE

HODDER AND STOUGHTON

NEW MATERIAL © ELIZABETH GOUDGE 1966
FIRST PRINTED 1966
THIS EDITION 1970
SECOND IMPRESSION 1971

ISBN 0 340 10559 3

Printed in Great Britain for Hodder and Stoughton Ltd,
St. Paul's House, Warwick Lane, London, E.C.4,
by Richard Clay (The Chaucer Press), Ltd, Bungay, Suffolk

FOR
SONIA HARWOOD

PREFACE

THESE prayers, a mixture of old and new, were not collected for literary merit, though some of the great prayers of the world are among them, but as practical help for a Christian still in the kindergarten of prayer. A proportion of them were collected over the years, with no thought of an eventual anthology, and so the sources were not always noted and it has not been easy to discover them. If mistakes have been made we would ask forgiveness for this. The prayers have been arranged in diary form, one or two for each day of the year, but because Christmas is the only great feast of the Church with a fixed date prayers for the other feasts will, I am afraid, need the help of the list of contents to find them. I would like to thank my friend Adelaide Makower for the help she has given me. I owe to her the Jewish prayers, and others which she found and sent to me.

CONTENTS

JANUARY

OUR DEDICATION OF OURSELVES
TO GOD AND HIS PRESENCE
WITH US
FOR THE CHURCH
IN DARKNESS AND TRIBULATION

HE whom I bow to only knows to whom I bow
When I attempt the ineffable Name, murmuring *Thou*,
And dream of Pheidian fancies and embrace in heart
Symbols (I know) which cannot be the thing Thou art.
Thus always, taken at their word, all prayers blaspheme
Worshipping with frail images a folk-lore dream,
And all men in their praying, self-deceived, address
The coinage of their own unquiet thoughts, unless
Thou in magnetic mercy to Thyself divert
Our arrows, aimed unskilfully, beyond desert;
And all men are idolators, crying unheard
To a deaf idol, if Thou take them at their word.

Take not, Oh Lord, our literal sense. Lord, in Thy great,
Unbroken speech our limping metaphor translate.

C. S. LEWIS
Poems

Our dedication of ourselves
to God and His presence
with us

January 1

NEW YEAR'S DAY

ETERNAL God, who makest all things new, and abidest
for ever the same: Grant us to begin this year in Thy
faith, and to continue it in Thy favour; that, guided in all
our doings, and guarded all our days, we may spend our
lives in Thy service, and finally, by Thy grace, attain the
glory of everlasting life; through Jesus Christ our Lord.

W. E. ORCHARD
Order of Divine Service for Public Worship

O Lord our God, great, eternal, wonderful in glory,
who keepest covenant and promise for those that love
Thee with their whole heart; we come before Thee in
this our new beginning, begging Thee to cleanse us from
our sins, and from every thought displeasing to Thy
goodness, that with a pure heart and a clear mind we
may venture confidently and fearlessly to pray unto
Thee; through Jesus Christ our Lord.

Liturgy of St. Basil
adapted

15

January 2

O LORD God, Holy Father . . . I am no longer my own,
but Thine. Put me to what Thou wilt, rank me with
whom Thou wilt; put me to doing, put me to suffering;
let me be employed for Thee or laid aside for Thee,
exalted for Thee or brought low for Thee; let me be full,
let me be empty; let me have all things, let me have
nothing; I freely and heartily yield all things to Thy
pleasure and disposal.

And now, O glorious and blessed God, Father, Son
and Holy Spirit, Thou art mine, and I am Thine. So be
it. And the Covenant which I have made on earth, let it
be ratified in heaven.

The Methodist Shorter Book of Offices

January 3

O LORD, our God! bless for us this year;
As also every kind of its produce for our benefit:
And bestow dew and rain for a blessing
Upon the face of the earth:
And water the face of the earth;
And satisfy the world with Thy goodness:
Replenish our hands with Thy blessings,
And with the rich gifts of Thy hands.
Protect and guard this year from all manner of evil,
And every form of calamity and destruction:
Cause our hope therein to be good,
So that it may end peacefully.

Jewish Prayer
Sephardi Prayer Book

ALMIGHTY God, who art beyond the reach of our highest thought, and yet within the heart of the lowliest; come to us, we pray Thee, in all the beauty of light, in all the tenderness of love, in all the liberty of truth. Mercifully help us to do justly, to love mercy, and to walk humbly with Thee. Sanctify all our desires and purposes, and upon each of us let Thy blessing rest; through Jesus Christ our Lord.

Service Book and Ordinal of the
Presbyterian Church of South Africa
adapted

WE beseech Thee, O Lord, mercifully to correct our wanderings; and by the guiding radiance of Thy compassion to bring us to the saving vision of Thy truth, through Jesus Christ our Lord.

Gothic Missal

Be Thou, O Lord, our Protector, who art our redemption; direct our minds by Thy gracious presence, and watch over our paths with guiding love; that, among the snares which lie hidden in this path wherein we walk, we may so pass onwards with hearts fixed on Thee, that by the track of faith we may come to be where Thou wouldest have us.

Mozarabic Liturgy

January 6: Epiphany

WHAT gift shall we bring to Thee, O Christ, since Thou as man on earth hast shown Thyself for us, since every creature made by Thee brings to Thee its thanksgiving? The angels bring their song, the Heavens bring their star, the Magi bring their gifts, the Shepherds bring their awe, earth gives a cave, the wilderness a manger: and we the Virgin Mother bring. God before all worlds, have mercy upon us!

First Vespers of Christmas in the Greek Church

January 7

ALMIGHTY Lord our God, direct our steps into the way of peace, and strengthen our hearts to obey Thy commandments; may the Day-spring visit us from on high, and give light to those who sit in darkness and the shadow of death; that they may adore Thee for Thy mercy, follow Thee for Thy truth, desire Thee for Thy sweetness, who art the blessed Lord God of Israel.

Ancient Collect

Almighty God, who hast planted the Day-star in the heavens, and, scattering the night, dost restore morning to the world, fill us, we beseech Thee, with Thy mercy, so that, Thou being our Enlightener, all the darkness of our sins may be dispersed, through our Lord Jesus Christ.

Sarum Breviary

January 8

O GOD, the protector of all that trust in Thee, without whom nothing is strong, nothing is holy, increase and multiply upon us Thy mercy; that, Thou being our Ruler and Guide, we may so pass through things temporal that we finally lose not the things eternal. Grant this, O heavenly Father, for Jesus Christ's sake our Lord.

Book of Common Prayer

January 9

O THOU, who fillest heaven and earth, ever acting, ever at rest, who art present everywhere and everywhere art wholly present, who art not absent even when far off, who with thy whole being fillest yet transcendest all things, who teachest the hearts of the faithful without the din of words; teach us, we pray Thee, through Jesus Christ our Lord.

ST. AUGUSTINE

January 10

O SAVIOUR Christ, who dost lead them to immortal blessedness, who commit themselves to Thee: Grant that we, being weak, presume not to trust in ourselves, but may always have Thee before our eyes, to follow Thee, our guide; that Thou, who only knowest the way, mayst lead us to our heavenly desires. To thee with the Father and the Holy Ghost be glory for ever.

Primer of 1559
adapted

19

For the Church

January 11

O MYSTERY, deep, unsearchable, eternal, which hast decked, with a splendid glory, the heavenly dominion, the legions of fiery spirits in the chamber of light unapproachable . . . Thou who didst spread Thy creating arms to the stars, strengthen our arms with power to intercede when we lift up our hands unto Thee. Supreme, divine Sovereign of all being, Thou hast covered us with a robe as with love, to be ministers of Thine holy mystery. O heavenly King, keep Thy Church immovable, and maintain in peace the worshippers of Thine Holy Name.

Armenian Prayer

January 12

BLESS, O Gracious Father, Thy holy Catholic Church. Fill it with truth and grace. When it is corrupt, purge it; when it is in error, direct it; when it is superstitious, rectify it; when it is amiss, reform it; when it is right, strengthen and confirm it; when it is divided and rent asunder, heal the breaches of it. O thou Holy One of Israel, bless all those who are called to any office or ministration in Thy Church; replenish them with the truth of Thy doctrine, and with integrity and innocence of life; remember all their offerings, and accept their burnt sacrifice. O Lord, let their prayers be precious in Thine ears, and the cries of all Thy people, even of the city of God, be not in vain.

ARCHBISHOP WILLIAM LAUD

O SOVEREIGN and Almighty Lord, bless all Thy people and all Thy flock. Give peace, Thy help, Thy love unto us, Thy servants, the sheep of Thy fold, that we may be united in the bond of peace and love, one body and one spirit, in one hope of our calling, in Thy divine and boundless love; for the sake of Jesus Christ, the great Shepherd of the sheep.

Liturgy of St. Mark

O GOD the Father, Fount of Godhead, good beyond all that is good, fair beyond all that is fair, in whom is calmness, peace, and concord; Do Thou make up the dissensions which divide Thy people, and bring us back into an unity of love, which may bear some likeness to Thy sublime nature. Grant this, O Father, through Thine only-begotten Son, that all we who have been redeemed by the mystery of His Incarnation may remain united in the fellowship of perpetual peace.

Jacobite Liturgy of St. Dionysius

January 15

O LORD Jesus Christ, who on the eve of Thy Passion didst pray that all Thy disciples might be one, as Thou art in the Father, and the Father in Thee, grant that we may suffer keenly on account of the infidelity of our disunion. Grant us the loyalty to recognize and the courage to reject all our hidden indifference and mistrust, and our mutual hostility.

Grant that we may find each other in Thee, so that from our hearts and from our lips may ceaselessly arise Thy prayer for the Unity of Christians, such as Thou willest and by the means that Thou willest. Grant that in Thee, who art perfect charity, we may find the way that leads to Unity, in obedience to Thy love and to Thy truth.

ABBÉ PAUL COUTURIER AND PÈRE MICHALON

January 16

O LORD, who willest that all Thy children should be one in Thee, we pray Thee for the unity of Thy Church. Pardon all our pride, and our lack of faith, of understanding and of charity, which are the cause of our divisions. Deliver us from our narrow-mindedness, from our bitterness, from our prejudices. Preserve us from considering as normal that which is a scandal to the world and an offence to Thy love. Teach us to recognize the gifts of Thy grace amongst all those who call upon Thee.

Liturgy of the Reformed Church of France

O LORD Jesus Christ, who at Thy first coming didst
send Thy messenger to prepare Thy way before Thee:
Grant that the ministers and stewards of Thy mysteries
may likewise so prepare and make ready Thy way, by
turning the hearts of the disobedient to the wisdom of
the just, that at Thy second coming to judge the world
we may be found an acceptable people in Thy sight,
who livest and reignest with the Father and the Holy
Spirit, ever one God, world without end.

Book of Common Prayer

O GOD our King and Saviour, look at this time in your
mercy upon the priests and ministers of Thy Church,
facing a world of danger and confusion, where faith
grows weak as doubts and sufferings increase. Grant to
them the outpouring of Thy Holy Spirit that Thy truth
may be made plain to them and Thy will shine clear,
their hearts know the strength of Thy courage and their
souls Thy peace. Lord, have mercy upon all Christian
people. Deepen our penitence, confirm our faith,
increase our love. Grant to a purged and united Church
that she may become, not in dream and hope only but
in very truth, the ark and refuge of mankind.

January 19

O GOD of all the nations of the earth, remember the multitudes of the heathen, who, though created in Thine image, have not known Thee, nor the dying of Thy Son their Saviour Jesus Christ; and grant that by the prayers and labours of Thy holy Church they may be brought from all ignorance and unbelief, and brought to worship Thee; through Him whom Thou hast sent to be the Resurrection and the Life of all men, the same Thy Son Jesus Christ our Lord.

ST. FRANCIS XAVIER

January 20

PRAYER OF THE DOVE

THE Ark waits,
Lord,
the Ark waits on Your will,
and the sign of Your peace.
I am the dove,
simple,
as the sweetness that comes from You.
The Ark waits,
Lord;
it has endured.
Let me carry it
a sprig of hope and joy,
and put, at the heart of its forsakenness,
this, in which Your love clothes me,
Grace immaculate.

CARMEN BERNOS DE GASZTOLD
Prayers from the Ark

In darkness and tribulation

OUT of the deep have I called unto Thee, O Lord, Lord, hear my voice.

O let Thine ears consider well the voice of my complaint.

If Thou, Lord, wilt be extreme to mark what is done amiss, O Lord, who may abide it?

For there is mercy with Thee, therefore shalt Thou be feared.

I look for the Lord; my soul doth wait for Him: in His word is my trust.

My soul fleeth unto the Lord before the morning watch, I say before the morning watch.

O Israel, trust in the Lord, for with the Lord there is mercy, and with Him is plenteous redemption.

And He shall redeem Israel from all his sins.

Psalm 130

AFORETIME in our distress, O Lord,
Thou wast wont to vouchsafe unto us Thy charity,
Thou didst hold our hands when they faltered;
Thou didst teach us, Do this and live.

But our overthrow came of a sudden,
And then were no hands to stay us.
Let healing come to the driven leaf.
Repent Thee concerning dust and ashes,
And cast our sins far away,
In pity for Thy handiwork.

See, we have none to intercede for us.
O deal Thou with us mercifully.

Jewish Prayer

O answer now the whisper of my prayer;
Be gracious to my cry,
Most holy God!

Jewish Prayer
Both from the *Service of the Orthodox Synagogue*
for the Day of Atonement

January 23

O GOD our Father, hear me, who am trembling in this darkness, and stretch forth Thy hand unto me; hold forth Thy light before me; recall me from my wanderings; and, Thou being my guide, may I be restored to myself and to Thee.

ST. AUGUSTINE

Lord, I am unable to stand under the cross, unable of myself, but be Thou pleased to ease this load by fortifying my spirit, that I may be strongest when I am weakest, and may be able to do and suffer everything that Thou pleasest, through Christ who strengthenest me.

JEREMY TAYLOR

January 24

O Thou great God enthroned,
    Succour me betimes with Thy goodness;
Make my sins unclean
    To part from me this night.

For mine afflictions forsake me not,
    For my tears' sake do not leave me!
Jesu! Thou likeness of the sun,
    In the day of my need be near me!

Leave me not in dumbness,
    Dead in the wilderness;
Leave me not to my stumbling,
    For my trust is in Thee, my Saviour!

Jesu, meet Thou my soul!
    Jesu, clothe me in Thy love!
Jesu, shield Thou my spirit!
    Jesu, stretch out to me Thine hand!
                    The Sun Dances
                    Prayers from the Gaelic

January 25

O Thou whose love to man was proven in the passion
and death of Jesus Christ our Lord, let the power
of His cross be with me to-day. Let me love as He loved.
Let my obedience be unto death. In leaning upon His
Cross, let me not refuse my own; yet in bearing mine,
let me bear it by the strength of His.

                    JOHN BAILLIE
                    A Diary of Private Prayer

27

January 26

THOU, who art the eternal protection and salvation of our souls, arm us, we entreat Thee, with the helmet of hope, and the shield of Thy invincible defence; that so, helped by Thee in the straits of our necessities, we may be filled with joy and gladness with those who love Thee, through Jesus Christ our Lord.

Sarum Breviary

January 27

O FATHER, help us to know that the hiding of Thy face is wise love. Thy love is not fond, doting and reasonless. Thy bairns must often have the frosty cold side of the hill, and set down both their bare feet amongst the thorns: Thy love hath eyes, and in the meantime is looking on. Our pride must have winter weather.

GEORGE MACDONALD

Lord, for the erring thought
Not into evil wrought:
Lord, for the wicked will
Betrayed and baffled still:
For the heart from itself kept,
Our thanksgiving accept.

For ignorant hopes that were
Broken to our blind prayer:
For pain, death, sorrow, sent
Unto our chastisement:
For all loss of seeming good,
Quicken our gratitude.

WILLIAM DEAN HOWELLS

January 28

O SAVIOUR Christ, we beseech Thee, when the wind is boisterous, and our faith weak, and we begin to sink even as we would fain come to Thee on the water, stretch forth Thy hand, O Lord, as of old to Thy fearful disciple, and say to the sea of our difficulties, Peace be still; for Thy holy Name's sake.

DEAN VAUGHAN

O Lord God, without whose will a sparrow doth not fall to the ground: Grant us in all trouble and adversity to be quiet, without impatience and without murmuring, with our whole trust and confidence in Thee, who workest all things for the best; to whom be glory for ever and ever.

Prayers of 1550

O MY God, Thou hast wounded me with love,
Behold the wound that is still vibrating,
O my God, Thou hast wounded me with love.

O my God, Thy fear hath fallen upon me,
Behold the burn is there, and it throbs aloud.
O my God, Thy fear hath fallen upon me.

O my God, I have known all that is vile,
And Thy glory hath stationed itself in me,
O my God, I have known all that is vile . . .

Take my blood that I have not poured out,
Take my flesh unworthy of Thy suffering,
Take my blood that I have not poured out . . .

Take my heart that has beaten for vain things,
To throb under the thorns of Calvary,
Take my heart that has beaten for vain things . . .

Ah, thou God of pardon and promises,
What is the pit of mine ingratitude!
Ah, thou God of pardon and promises.

God of terror and God of holiness,
Alas, my sinfulness is a black abyss,
God of terror and holiness.

Thou God of peace, of joy and delight,
All my tears, all my ignorances,
Thou God of peace, of joyous delight.

Thou, God, knowest all this, all this,
How poor I am, poorer than any man,
Thou, O God, knowest all this, all this.

And what I have, my God, I give to Thee.

PAUL VERLAINE
Translated by Arthur Symons

January 30

PRAYER OF THE GLOW-WORM

DEAR God,
would You take Your Light
a little farther away
from me?
I am like a morsel
of cinder
and need Your night
for my heart to dare
to flicker out its feeble star:
its hope, to give to other hearts,
what can be stolen from all poverty—
a gleam of joy.

CARMEN BERNOS DE GASZTOLD
Prayers from the Ark

January 31

O GOD, the might of all them that put their trust in Thee; Grant that we may be more than conquerors over all that makes war upon our souls, and in the end may enter into perfect peace in Thy presence; through Jesus Christ our Lord.

Roman Breviary

O praise our God, ye people, and make the voice of His praise to be heard;

Who holdeth our soul on life and suffereth not our feet to slip.

For Thou, O God, hast proved us: Thou also hast tried us, like as silver is tried . . . we went through fire and water, and Thou broughtest us out into a wealthy place . . .

O come hither, and hearken, all ye that fear God, and I will tell you what He hath done for my soul . . .

Praised be God who hath not cast out my prayer nor turned His mercy from me.

Psalm 66

FEBRUARY

SEEKING AND LONGING FOR GOD

FOR THOSE WHO SUFFER IN ILLNESS

THE WILL OF GOD, AND OUR WORK

LORD of the world, He reigned alone
  While yet the universe was naught.
  When by His will all things were wrought,
Then first His sovran Name was known.

And when the All shall cease to be,
  In dread lone splendour He shall reign.
  He was, He is, He shall remain
In glorious eternity.

For He is one, no second shares
  His nature or His loneliness;
  Unending and beginningless,
All strength is His, all sway He bears.

He is the living God to save,
  My Rock while sorrow's toils endure,
  My banner and my stronghold sure,
The cup of life whene'er I crave.

I place my soul within His palm
  Before I sleep as when I wake,
  And though my body I forsake,
Rest in the Lord in fearless calm.

Jewish hymn
attributed to SOLOMON IBN GABRIOL
11th century

Seeking and longing for God

February 1

LIKE as the hart desireth the waterbrooks, so longeth my soul after Thee, O God.

My soul is athirst for God, yea, even for the living God: when shall I come to appear before the presence of God?

Psalm 42

O God, Thou art my God, early will I seek Thee.

My soul thirsteth for Thee, my flesh also longeth after Thee, in a barren and dry land where no water is.

For Thy loving-kindness is better than life itself: my lips shall praise Thee.

Have I not remembered Thee in my bed, and thought upon Thee when I was waking?

Because Thou hast been my helper, therefore under the shadow of Thy wings will I rejoice.

Psalm 63

February 2

THOU brightness of eternal glory, Thou comforter of the pilgrim soul, with Thee is my tongue without voice, and my very silence speaketh unto Thee. Come, oh, come; for without Thee I shall have no joyful day or hour; for Thou art my joy, and without Thee my table is empty. Praise and glory be unto Thee; let my mouth, my soul, and all creatures together, praise and bless Thee.

THOMAS À KEMPIS

And I talked with you as friends talk, my glory and my riches and my Salvation, my Lord God . . . O Thou, the Power of my soul, enter into it and fit it for Thyself, that Thou mayest have it and possess it without spot or wrinkle. This is my hope, this is my prayer.

ST. AUGUSTINE
Confessions

February 3

THYSELF, O my God, Thyself for Thine own sake
     above all things I love.
Thyself as my last end I long for.
Make me therefore in this life present alway
     to love Thee before all things,
     to seek Thee in all things,
and at the last in the life to come
     to find and to keep Thee for ever.

THOMAS BRADWARDINE
Archbishop of Canterbury

O Eternal Light, shine in our hearts,
O Eternal Goodness, deliver us from evil,
O Eternal Power, be our support,
O Eternal Wisdom, scatter our darkness,
O Eternal Pity, have mercy upon us;
that with all our heart and mind and soul and strength we may seek Thy face and be brought by Thine infinite mercy to Thy holy presence; through Jesus Christ Our Lord.

ALEVIN

February 4

WE praise Thee, O unseen Father, giver of immortality. Thou art the fount of life, the fount of light, the fount of all grace and all truth, O lover of men, O lover of the poor, who dost reconcile Thyself to all, and draw all to Thyself through the coming of Thy beloved Son. We beseech Thee, make us living men. Give us a spirit of light that we may know Thee, the True, and Him whom Thou didst send, Jesus Christ. Give us this Holy Spirit, that we may be able to tell forth and declare Thine ineffable mysteries. May the Lord Jesus speak in us, and the Holy Spirit hymn Thee through us.

Sacramentary of Sarepion

February 5

OPEN our eyes, O Lord of all goodness, that they may see Thy ways, who hast prepared ours from all eternity; and our hearts that they may learn of Thine, who, when Thou lovest, lovest to the end; through Jesus Christ our Lord.

ERIC MILNER-WHITE
A Cambridge Bede Book

February 6

BY the forgiving tenderness, O Lord, wherewith Thou didst ever wait for us; by that tender love wherewith whenever we wandered, Thou didst watch over us; by Thine infinite love wherewith Thou willest that we

should love Thee eternally; Give us love like Thine,
that we may grow in Thy love, and dwelling in love may
dwell in Thee.

EDWARD BOUVERIE PUSEY

February 7

You, God of my Love, are the Life of souls, the Life of
lives, Livingness itself, and You shall not change, O
Life of my soul.

ST. AUGUSTINE
Confessions

We are the mediocre,
we are the half givers,
we are the half lovers,
we are the savourless salt.
Lord Jesus Christ,
restore us now,
to the primal splendour
of first love.
To the austere light
of the breaking day.
Let us hunger and thirst,
let us burn in the flame.
Break the hard crust
of complacency.
Quicken in us
the sharp grace of desire.

CARYLL HOUSELANDER
The Flowering Tree

AND if still I cannot find Thee, O God, then let me
search my heart and know whether it is not rather I
who am blind than Thou who art obscure, and I who
am fleeing from Thee rather than Thou from me;
and let me confess these my sins before Thee and seek
Thy pardon in Jesus Christ my Lord.

JOHN BAILLIE
A Diary of Private Prayer

Our God, it is Thy will in us that willeth.

It is Thy desire in us that desireth.

It is Thy urge in us that would turn our nights,
which are Thine, into days, which are Thine also.

We cannot ask Thee for aught, for Thou knowest our
needs before they are born in us:

Thou art our need; and in giving us more of Thyself
Thou givest us all.

KAHLIL GIBRAN
The Prophet

MY spirit longs for Thee
    Within my troubled breast,
Though I unworthy be
    Of so divine a Guest.

Of so divine a Guest
   Unworthy though I be,
Yet has my heart no rest
   Unless it come from Thee.

Unless it come from Thee,
   In vain I look around;
In all that I can see
   No rest is to be found.

No rest is to be found
   But in Thy blessèd love:
O, let my wish be crowned,
   And send it from above!

J. BYROM

February 10

God be in my head
And in my understanding.
God be in mine eyes
And in my looking.
God be in my mouth
And in my speaking.
God be in my heart
And in my thinking.
God be at mine end
And at my departing.

Sarum Primer 1527

Thine are goodness, grace, love, kindness, O Thou Lover of men! Gentleness, tenderness, forbearance, long-suffering, manifold mercies, great mercies, abundant tender compassions. Glory be to Thee, O Lord.

LANCELOT ANDREWES
The Private Prayers of Lancelot Andrewes

For those who suffer in illness

February 11

ALMIGHTY and everlasting God, who canst banish all affliction both of soul and body; show forth the power of Thine aid upon those who are sick, that by the help of Thy mercy they may be restored to serve Thee afresh in holiness of living; through Jesus Christ our Lord.

Gelasian Sacramentary

O Thou who art the Healer of all flesh
  And bindest up their wounds,
Send a perfect healing from heaven,
  A healing of soul and body,
Unto all who lie on a bed of pain in our city.
Turn their weakness into strength,
  And bless them with bodily vigour;
Restore them to perfect health.
  And prolong their days in happiness and well-being;
  And let us say, Amen.

Jewish Prayer
Authorized Daily Prayer Book

February 12

FOR THOSE WHO SUFFER IN SEVERE ILLNESS

OUR Saviour Christ, your love for us passes knowledge, yet kneeling before your cross we see and know that the suffering we inflicted upon you there is turned by the glory of your love into blessing for us. Your woe is our

42

weal, your death our life, and by your stripes we are healed. Remembering this, we humbly pray for those who in illness suffer the same fear, pain and exhaustion that you knew in your passion, knowing it for their sakes, that in suffering they might be one with you in the greatest hour of your redeeming love. We pray for them that this union with you may be revealed to them in an increase of courage and strength. We pray that if it be Thy will healing may come to them with all the joy of your resurrection, but that whether in life or death your love may be made known to them and your peace bless them for ever.

February 13

FOR THE CRIPPLED

O LORD Jesus Christ, bound to the pillar and nailed to the cross, we pray to Thee for those who have lost their physical freedom and can no longer walk with other men and share their work and joy. We pray for those who lie in iron lungs, and all held captive by crippling diseases, all injured in accidents or maimed by war. We remember the young, and we remember too those who have spent many years in pain and weariness. Grant, O Lord, that we who have our freedom may never forget them but may have them always in our hearts and prayers. Knowing ourselves incapable of their courage and cheerfulness, we ask with humility and reverence that the bestowals of your grace may come to them with increasing blessing. Lord, illumine their fortitude and patience with your own, uphold them in your love and possess them with your peace.

February 14

FOR THE MENTALLY ILL

O GOD of light and peace, give light and peace to them
that are of a troubled mind; Grant them courage and
patience, that they may seek for the causes of their ills;
and give wisdom to those who help them to do so. And,
for those whose sufferings continue, we pray that they
may be cared for in love, and that none may add to their
griefs. We ask this in the name of him who succoured
the distressed, Thy Son, Jesus Christ our Lord.

Anon.

FOR THE NERVOUSLY ILL

Lord of great compassion, we pray to you for those who
are nervously ill, and too weak and anxious to lift
themselves above the fear and sadness that threaten to
overwhelm them. Do you yourself, O Lord, lift them up
and deliver them, as you delivered your disciples in the
storm at sea, strengthening their faith and banishing
their fear. Turning to you, O Lord, may they find you,
and finding you may they find also all that you have
laid up for them within the safe fortress of your love and
peace.

FOR THE BLIND

O LORD Jesus Christ, blindfolded as the sun rose upon the day of your passion, so that you could not tell who it was that struck you, knowing only that it was those you loved, we pray to you for the blind who may no longer look upon the beauty of this world or the faces of their friends. Lord in your mercy grant them increasing awareness of the other world, of which this of our senses is no more than a shadow or reflection, and of yourself, Light of all worlds, Light of God, friend and Saviour of our souls, whom to seek is mercy and to find is rest.

FOR THE DEAF

We pray to Thee, O Lord, for those who are deaf and can no longer hear the birds singing, the music of stringed instruments and all the many voices of the world. We beseech Thee, turn the colours of the world into singing for them, and the order of it to melodious harmony. Lord, deliver their silence from emptiness and grant that they may find within it the fullness of your love.

February 16

FOR SICK AND CRIPPLED CHILDREN

O MOST loving Lord, you who know all things know that nothing weighs more heavily on our hearts and minds than the suffering of sick or crippled children. If sinners can so grieve, O Lord, what can this grief be for you in the perfection of your love? As you bore our sins, so you bear our sorrows, and would receive our prayers too into your heart, to become a part of your love that is forever working for us in ways we do not understand, but in ways that we trust and adore. Lord, strengthen, bless and direct all the labour, all the prayer, and all the love that is poured out upon children who suffer, and grant that there may be no heart left that is unconcerned for them, and no mind unresolved to make of this sinful world a safer and happier home for them.

February 17

FOR THE DYING

O SAVIOUR of the world, lifted upon the cross that all men might be drawn to your love, dying for the salvation of us all, we beseech Thee to make that love and that salvation a growing reality of glory to those who face their death. Grant to them, O Lord, Thy gift of a perfect repentance, and then may the heaven of Thy forgiveness banish all fears from them forever.

O Lord we beseech Thee,
who art the succour of the succourless,
   the hope of them that are past hope,
   the saviour of the tempest-tossed,
   the harbour of the voyagers,
   the physician of the sick;
Thyself become all things to all men,
   who knowest each one and his petition,
   each house and its need.
And receive us all into Thy kingdom
   making us children of light;
and Thy peace and love bestow upon us,
   O Lord our God.

Liturgy of St. Basil

The will of God, and our work

February 19

GOD Almighty, Eternal, Righteous, and Merciful, give to us poor sinners to do for Thy sake all that we know of Thy will, and to will always what pleases Thee, so that inwardly purified, enlightened, and kindled by the fire of the Holy Spirit, we may follow in the footprints of Thy well-beloved Son, our Lord Jesus Christ.

ST. FRANCIS OF ASSISI

February 20

LORD, help us to accomplish Thy Divine Will, in whatever manner you may wish to be served by us in this world; using diligence to keep ourselves peaceful and tranquil, taking everything from the Hand of our Heavenly Father, for in your Hand alone is the cup from which we have to drink.

JOHN OF BONELLA
adapted

February 21

O GOD, who hast made of all those who are born again in Christ a royal and a priestly race, give us the will and the power to do what Thou commandest; that Thy people, being called into eternity, may have one faith in their hearts and one law in their lives.

Gregorian Sacramentary

LORD, we know not what we ought to ask of Thee;
Thou only knowest what we need, Thou lovest us better
than we know how to love ourselves. O Father, give to
us, Thy children, that which we ourselves know not how
to ask. We would have no other desire than to accomplish Thy will. Teach us to pray. Pray Thyself in us; for
Christ's sake.

FRANÇOIS FÉNELON
adapted

February 23

O GOD who hast ordained that whatever is to be
desired, should be sought by labour, and who, by Thy
blessing, bringest honest labour to good effect; look with
mercy upon my studies and endeavours. Grant me, O
Lord, to design only what is lawful and right; and afford
me calmness of mind, and steadiness of purpose, that I
may so do Thy will in this short life, as to obtain happiness in the world to come, for the sake of Jesus Christ
our Lord.

SAMUEL JOHNSON

February 24

O GOD, renew our spirits by Thy Holy Spirit, and draw our hearts unto Thyself, that our work may not be a burden, but a delight. Let us not serve as slaves with the spirit of bondage, but with freedom and gladness as Thy sons, rejoicing in Thy will; for Jesus Christ's sake.

BENJAMIN JENKS

Stir us up to offer to Thee, O Lord, our bodies, our souls, our spirits, in all we love and all we learn, in all we plan and all we do, to offer our labours, our pleasures, our sorrows to Thee; to work through them for Thy Kingdom, to live as those who are not their own, but bought with Thy blood, fed with Thy body; Thine from our birth-hour, Thine now, and Thine for ever and ever.

CHARLES KINGSLEY

LORD, teach us to work with love, knowing that work is love made visible.

Teach us to weave the cloth with threads drawn from our heart, even as if you our beloved were to wear that cloth.

To build a house with affection, even as if you were to dwell in that house.

To sow seeds with tenderness and reap the harvest with joy, even as if you were to eat the fruit.

To charge all things we fashion with a breath of our own spirit,

And to know that all the blessed dead are standing about us and watching.

KAHLIL GIBRAN
The Prophet
adapted

February 26

BEFORE STARTING ANY WORK

LORD, in union with the love which made Thee deign to occupy Thyself in work . . . I beg Thee to unite my work with Thy most perfect acts and make it perfect; as a drop of water, poured into a great river, does all that river does.

Lord, I desire that, at all times, those who profit by my labour may be not only refreshed in body, but may be also drawn to Thy love and strengthened in every good.

Both from The True Prayers of St. Gertrude
and St. Mechtilde

February 27

O LORD, Thou knowest how busy I must be this day. If I forget Thee, do not forget me.

JACOB ASTLEY
Before the battle of Edgehill

O Lord God, when Thou givest to Thy servants to endeavour any great matter, grant us to know that it is not the beginning but the continuing of the same, until it be thoroughly finished, which yieldeth the true glory.

SIR FRANCIS DRAKE

Keep us, Lord, so awake in the duties of our calling that we may sleep in Thy peace and wake in Thy glory.

JOHN DONNE

PRAYERS OF TWO WORKERS

The Bee

LORD,
I am not one to despise your gifts.
May you be blessed
who spread the riches of your sweetness
for my zeal . . .
Let my small span of ardent life
melt into our great communal task;
to lift up to your glory
this temple of sweetness,
a citadel of incense,
a holy candle, myriad-celled,
moulded of your graces
and of the hidden work.

The Ox

Dear God, give me time.
Men are always so driven!
Make them understand that I can never hurry.
Give me time to eat.
Give me time to plod.
Give me time to sleep.
Give me time to think.

CARMEN BERNOS DE GASZTOLD
Prayers from the Ark

MARCH

IN PRAISE OF CHRIST OUR LORD

PENITENCE

THE CROSS

When Christ came from the shadows by the stream
Of Phlegethon,
Scars were upon His feet, His hands, His side.
Not, as dulled souls might deem,
That He who had the power
Of healing all the wounds whereof men died
Could not have healed His own,
But that those scars had some divinity,
Carriage of mystery,
Life's source to bear the stigmata of death . . .

By these same scars, in prayer for all mankind,
Before His Father's face
He pleads our wounds within His mortal flesh,
And all the Travail of His mortal days,
For ever interceding for His grace,
Remembering where forgetfulness were blind,
For ever pitiful, for ever kind,
Instant that Godhead should take thought for man,
Remembering the manhood of His Son,
His only Son, and the deep wounds He bore.

By these same scars His folk will not give o'er
Office of worship, while they see,
Passion, Thy mystery;
In those dark wounds, their weal,
In that descent to hell their climb to the stars,
His death, their life;
Their wreath, His crown of thorns.

THEODULF
a judge under Charlemagne

In praise of Christ our Lord

ALL hail! the worship of the world, the mirror of saints, whom spirits of heaven covet for to see. Cleanse us from every spot of vice and join us to the fellowship of blessed men. All hail! our joy in this hard life, sliding and fragile, soon for to pass . . . Lead us to a country, to Christ's face to be seen, that is full clear. We beseech Thee, be to us a siker helper, a sweet defender, and a counsellor, that a grievous enemy noye us not, but enjoy we rest. All folks say they: "So be it."

MS University College

SACRIFICES of praise may we be accounted worthy to offer unto Thee, O Lord, a sweet-smelling savour, even all our thoughts and words and deeds and holocausts, and without spot to appear before Thee all the days of our life.

Greek Church

O Holy Jesus, most merciful
Redeemer, Friend and Brother,
May I see Thee more clearly,
Love Thee more dearly, and
Follow Thee more nearly,
Day by day.

ST. RICHARD OF CHICHESTER

March 3

I SAY the prayer from my mouth,
I say the prayer from my heart,
I say the prayer to Thee Thyself,
   O Healing Hand, O Son of the God
     of Salvation;
To give praise to Thee, Jesus,
Lord of sea and of land,
Lord of sun and of moon,
   Lord of the beautiful stars.

O God of the weak,
O God of the lowly,
O God of the righteous,
   O shield of homesteads:

Thou art calling upon us
In the voice of glory,
With the mouth of mercy
   Of Thy beloved Son.

O may I find rest everlasting
In the home of Thy Trinity,
In the Paradise of the godly,
   In the Sun-garden of Thy love.

The Sun Dances
Prayers from the Gaelic

GOOD and great God! How should I fear
To come to Thee, if Christ not there!
Could I but think, He would not be
Present, to plead my cause for me;
To Hell I'd rather run, than I
Would see Thy face, and He not by.

ROBERT HERRICK

LOVE, thou didst enter very softly in
   To hold this heart of mine.
   No sound, no stir, no sign!
How couldst thou cross my threshold all unseen?

O Love, thou fire divine, of laughter spun;
   Love that art smile and jest,
   Thou giv'st us of thy best,
Thy wealth unmeasured that is never done.

O sweet and gentle Love, thou art the key
   Of heaven's city and fort:
   Steer thou my ship to port,
And from the tempest's fury shelter me.

JACOPONE DA TODI

March 6

O LORD Jesus Christ, who art the very bright Sun of the world, ever rising, never going down: Shine, we beseech Thee, upon our spirit, that the night of sin and error being driven away by Thy inward light, we may walk without stumbling, as in the day. Grant this, O Lord, who livest and reignest with the Father and the Holy Ghost for evermore.

Primer of 1559

To Thee, O Jesu, I direct my eyes;
To Thee my hands, to Thee my humble knees;
To Thee my heart shall offer sacrifice;
To Thee my thoughts, who my thoughts only sees;
To Thee my self—my self and all I give;
To Thee I die; to Thee I only live.

Attributed to SIR WALTER RALEIGH

March 7

SAVIOUR, I know that none other
Stumbled before Thee as I stumbled,
Or did the deeds which I wrought.
But this too I know,
That the greatness of my stumblings
And the multitude of my sins
Go not beyond the measure
Of the long-suffering of my God,
Beyond the height of his loving-kindness.
These things make me to venture;
These things give me wings, O my Christ.

Therefore giving thanks in mind,
Giving thanks in heart,
Giving thanks in the members
Of my soul and of my body,
I worship Thee, I magnify Thee,
I glorify Thee, my God
That art blessed
Now and for evermore.

Greek Hieratikon

March 8

JESUS, preaching good tidings to the poor,
    proclaiming release to the captives,
    setting at liberty them that are bound,
                        I adore Thee.

Jesus, Friend of the poor,
    Feeder of the hungry,
    Healer of the sick,
                        I adore Thee.

Jesus, denouncing the oppressor,
    instructing the simple,
    going about doing good,
                        I adore Thee.

Jesus, Teacher of patience,
    Pattern of gentleness,
    Prophet of the kingdom of heaven,
                        I adore Thee.

A Book of Prayers for Students

March 9

O LORD Jesus Christ, who hast said that Thou art the way, the truth, and the life; Suffer us not at any time to stray from Thee, who art the way; nor to distrust Thy promises, who art the truth; nor to rest in any other thing than Thee, who art the life; beyond which there is nothing to be desired, neither in heaven, nor in earth; for Thy Name's sake.

A Booke of Christian Prayers, 1578

O Master Christ!
Thou hast loved us with an everlasting love:
Thou hast forgiven us, trained us, disciplined us:
Thou hast broken us loose and laid Thy commands upon us:
Thou hast set us in the thick of things and deigned to use us:
Thou hast shown Thyself to us, fed us, guided us:
Be graciously pleased to accept and forgive our poor efforts,
And keep us Thy free bondslaves for ever.

Anon.

O GOD, I love Thee, I love Thee—
Not out of hope of heaven for me
Nor fearing not to love and be
   In the everlasting burning.
Thou, Thou, my Jesus, after me
   Didst reach Thine arms out dying,
For my sake sufferedst nails and lance,
Mocked and marred countenance,
   Sorrows passing number,
   Sweat and care and cumber,
Yea and death, and this for me,
   And Thou couldst see me sinning:
Then I, why should I not love Thee,
Jesu, so much in love with me?
Not for heaven's sake; not to be
Out of hell by loving Thee;
Not for any gains I see;
But just the way that Thou didst me
I do love and I will love Thee:
What must I love Thee, Lord, for then?
For being my king and God. Amen.

                GERARD MANLEY HOPKINS

March 11

O MY Creator!
Consume the thorns of all my offences.
Make clean my soul, make holy my mind,
Nail down my being in Thy fear,
Ever keep watch, guard and protect me
From every act and word that destroyeth the soul.
Make me holy, make me clean, set me in order.
Make me comely, give me understanding, give me light.
Show me as the tabernacle of Thy Spirit alone,
And no more the tabernacle of sin,
And make Thy slave a child of light.
For it is Thou that makest holy, and we know none other
    that is good but Thee;
Thou art the shining brightness of souls
And to Thee, as is justly due, as God and Master,
We all give glory every day.

SIMEON THE TRANSLATOR
Greek Hieratikon

WE beseech Thee, supreme King of kings, great, mighty
and tremendous God, that it be in Thy grace to
comfort us and to purify us of all our transgressions
and sins.

O look down upon us from Thy dwelling place, even from
Heaven, and from there pour forth forgiveness upon
Thy servant who now prostrates himself before Thee,
so that Thou prolong his days and pardon his sins, his
iniquities and transgressions.

Stretch out Thy right hand to receive him in perfect
repentance, and open Thy good treasure to satisfy the
thirsting soul.

Jewish Prayer
Service of the Orthodox Synagogue for the
Festival of Tabernacles

March 13

O OUR God . . . it would go ill with the most praise-
worthy life lived by men, if you were to examine it with
your mercy laid aside! . . . Our one hope, our one
confidence, our one firm promise is your mercy.

ST. AUGUSTINE
Confessions

O Lord, who hast mercy upon all, take away from me my sins, and mercifully kindle in me the fire of Thy Holy Spirit. Take away from me the heart of stone, and give me a heart of flesh, a heart to love and adore Thee, a heart to delight in Thee, to follow and to enjoy Thee, for Christ's sake.

ST. AMBROSE

March 14

GOOD Jesu, God's Son, knower of all things, help me in wicked thoughts, that I displease Thee not . . . Courteous Jesu, when Thy will is, put them away and take me to Thy grace.

Jesu Christ, God's Son, which stood still before the judge nothing answering, withdraw my tongue till I think what and how I shall speak that may be to Thy worship.

Jesu Christ, God's Son, whose hands were bound for my love full sore, govern and teach mine hands and all mine other limbs that all my works may begin and graciously end to Thy most pleasing.

A Priest's Prayer
Bodleian MS

GOD of charity and peace, who dost bow Thyself down
to the prayers of those that abase themselves, have pity
on us. Hearken unto us. Abate the fury of the tempests
that assail us, and give unto us the peace of Thy tranquillity. And if through the multitude of our sins we have lost
it, give it to us again through Thy pitiful mercy.

Gothic Missal

March 16

O LORD my God, when sore bested
　　My evil life I do bewail,
What times the life I might have led
　　Arising smites me like a flail:

When I regard the past of sin,
　　Till sorrow drowns me like despair;
The saint in me that might have been
　　With what I am when I compare:

Then grant the life that might have been
　　To be in fact through penitence;
All my past years discharged of sin,
　　And spent in grace and innocence:

And grant that I, when I fore cast,
　　And shrink in fear of coming things,
May take this comfort of the past,
　　And lay it on my imaginings.

RICHARD WATSON DIXON
Hymn in *Posthumous Poems*

March 17

I HAVE deferred repentance, and Thou hast prolonged patience, O Thou that art mercy, Thou that art a fountain inexhaustible.

LANCELOT ANDREWES
The Private Prayers of Lancelot Andrewes

O everlasting God, let the light of Thine eternity now fall upon my passing days. O holy God, let the light of Thy perfect righteousness fall upon my sinful ways. O most merciful God, let the light of Thy love pierce to the most secret corners of my heart and overcome the darkness of sin within me.

JOHN BAILLIE
A Diary of Private Prayer

March 18

TIMES without number have I pray'd,
"This only once forgive";
Relapsing, when Thy hand was stay'd,
And suffer'd me to live:—

Yet now the kingdom of Thy peace,
Lord, to my heart restore;
Forgive my vain repentances,
And bid me sin no more.

CHARLES WESLEY

O LORD Jesus Christ, Son of the living God, grant us of Thy tender grace true fellowship with Thee in Thy sufferings, by abhorring and renouncing the open sins and the secret sins, the habitual sins and the sudden sins, the little sins and the great sins, which crucify Thee afresh; who now livest and reignest with the Father and the Holy Ghost, for ever and ever.

ERIC MILNER-WHITE
A Procession of Passion Prayers

LORD Jesus Christ! A whole life long didst Thou suffer that I too might be saved; and yet Thy suffering is not yet at an end; but this too wilt Thou endure, saving and redeeming me, this patient suffering of having to do with me, I who so often go astray from the right path, or even when I remained on the straight path stumbled along it or crept so slowly along the right path. Infinite patience, suffering of infinite patience. How many times have I not been impatient, wished to give up and forsake everything; wished to take the terribly easy way out, despair: but Thou didst not lose patience. Oh, I cannot say what Thy chosen servant says: that he filled up that which is behind of the afflictions of Christ in his flesh; no, I can only say that I increased Thy sufferings, added new ones to those which Thou didst once suffer in order to save me.

KIERKEGAARD
Journals

The Cross

March 21

O LOVING Saviour, we would linger by Thy Cross, that the light of Thy perfect love may shine into the secret places of our souls, showing what is vile there, so that it may shrink away; and nurturing whatever there is pure or lovely or of good report, so that beholding Thee, we may become more like Thee, Thou Revealer of God to men, Thou Guide of men to God.

WILLIAM TEMPLE

March 22

ALMIGHTY God, whose most dear Son went not up to joy but first He suffered pain, and entered not into glory before He was crucified; Mercifully grant that we, walking in the way of the Cross, may find it none other than the way of life and peace; through the same Thy Son Jesus Christ our Lord.

WILLIAM REED-HUNTINGDON
Book of Common Prayer
Protestant Episcopal Church in the U.S.A.

O Lord Jesus, forasmuch as Thy life was despised by the world, grant us so to imitate Thee, though the world despise, and with Thy image always before our eyes, to learn that only the servants of the Cross can find the way of blessedness and of true light. Hear us and save us, Lord Christ.

THOMAS À KEMPIS

O LORD Jesus Christ, Son of the living God, set Thine holy Passion, Cross and Death between Thy judgement and our souls, both now and in the hour of death. And vouchsafe, we beseech Thee, to grant unto the living mercy and grace, to the dead pardon and rest, to thine holy Church peace and concord, and to us miserable sinners life and joy everlasting; who livest and reignest with the Father and the Holy Ghost, one God, world without end.

Prayer of 1559

March 24

O LORD Jesus Christ, who hast given Thy life to redeem me, Thy-self for my example, Thy word for my rule, Thy grace for my guide, Thy body on the cross for the sin of my soul: Enter in and take possession of my heart, and dwell with me for ever.

After JEREMY TAYLOR

O Lamb of God,
that takest away the sins of the world,
Have mercy on us.
Thou that takest away the sins of the world,
Have mercy on us.
Thou that takest away the sins of the world,
Receive our prayer.
Thou that sittest at the right hand of God the Father,
Have mercy on us.

From *Gloria in Excelsis*

March 25: Palm Sunday

O LORD, our good Redeemer, who dost draw near to the passion of our redemption, a gentle rider on a gentle beast, Thy path thickly strewn with branches, and palms of triumph waved for Thee together with the uplifted voice of praise: we beseech Thy Divine Majesty to be pleased to receive the homage of our lips and the subjection of our bodies unto fasting. And grant that we may bring forth fruit to perfection; that, even as these came forth to meet Thee bearing branches of trees, so we, when Thou dost come again in Thy glory, may be found worthy to run before Thee with gladness, bearing the palms of victory in our hands.

Gothic Missal

March 26: Monday in Holy Week

ALMIGHTY and everlasting God, who, of Thy tender love towards mankind, hast sent Thy Son, our Saviour Jesus Christ, to take upon Him our flesh, and to suffer death upon the cross, that all mankind should follow the example of His great humility; Mercifully grant, that we may both follow the example of His patience, and also be made partakers of His resurrection; through the same Jesus Christ our Lord.

Book of Common Prayer

March 27: Tuesday in Holy Week

O LORD God, whose blessed Son, our Saviour, gave His back to the smiters and hid not His face from shame; Grant us grace to take joyfully the sufferings of the present time, in full assurance of the glory that shall be revealed; through the same Thy Son Jesus Christ our Lord.

Book of Common Prayer
Protestant Episcopal Church in the U.S.A.

March 28: Wednesday in Holy Week

O GOD, eternal Might, hasten unto us. Thou, who by Thy power makest things future to be as things past, and also by Thy presence, things past to be as things present; grant that Thy Passion may be as saving to us as if it were present this day: Thou who reignest forever with the Father and the Holy Ghost, now begin to reign over us, Man, God, Christ Jesus, King for ever and ever.

Mozarabic Liturgy
adapted

March 29: Maundy Thursday

Soul of Christ sanctify us:
Body of Christ save us:
Blood of Christ refresh us:
Water from the side of Christ wash us:
Passion of Christ strengthen us:
O Good Jesus, hear us:
Within Thy wounds hide us:
Suffer us not to be separated from Thee:
From the malicious enemy defend us:
In the hour of our death call us,
And bid us come to Thee.
That with Thy saints we may praise Thee
For ever and ever.

Anon.

May the sacred feast of Thy table, O Lord, always
strengthen and renew us, guide and protect our weakness
amid the storms of the world, and bring us into the haven
of everlasting salvation; through Jesus Christ our Lord.

Leonine Sacramentary

March 30: Good Friday

BLESSED be Thy name, O Jesu, Son of the most high God; blessed be the sorrow Thou sufferedst when Thy holy hands and feet were nailed to the tree; and blessed Thy love when, the fullness of pain accomplished, Thou didst give Thy soul into the hands of the Father; so by Thy Cross and precious Blood redeeming all the world, all longing souls departed and the numberless unborn; who now livest and reignest in the glory of the eternal Trinity for ever and ever.

From JEREMY TAYLOR

O praise God in His holiness, praise Him in the firmament of His power.

Praise Him in His noble acts, praise Him according to His excellent greatness.

Let everything that hath breath praise the Lord.

Psalm 150

March 31: Easter Eve

THOU, the Life, wert laid in the grave, O Christ; and the hosts of the angels shuddered, praising Thy humility.

Ritual of the Orthodox Church

O holy Jesus Christ, grant us so to perfect our repentance that our sins may be buried in Thy grave; and prepare our hearts to greet Thee with loving joy on the morning of Thy resurrection, Who didst die and wast buried and didst rise again for us, our only Lord and Saviour.

Anon.

It is meet and right, holy Father, Almighty, Eternal God, at all times to give praise to Thy goodness; but on this night and day the more abundantly, from souls exulting in joy. For this night is the mother not of darkness but of light, whereon day rose for ever; even our resurrection, the Lord Jesus Christ.

Mozarabic Missal

APRIL

EASTER

THE GLORY OF THE WORLD

FOR OUR FRIENDS

THIS morning, lying couched amid the grass
In the deep, deep dingle south of Llangwyth's Pass,
   While it was yet neither quite bright nor dark,
I heard a new and wonderful High Mass.
   The Chief Priest was the nightingale: the lark
And thrush assisted him: and some small bird
   (I do not weet his name) acted as Clerk.
My spirit was lapped in ecstasy: each word,
Word after word, thrilled through me like the deep
Rich music of a dream: not wholly asleep
Nor all awake was I, but, as it were
   Tranced somewhere between one state and the other.
   All heavy thoughts that through the long day smother
Man's heart and soul with weariness and care
   Were gone, and in their place reigned pure delight.
   The nightingale, sent from a far and bright
Land by my golden sister, prophesied
   Of blessèd days to come, in a sweet voice:
   And the small bird, responding, sang "Rejoice,
   rejoice!"
I heard his little bill tinkle and jingle
With a clear silver sound that filled the dingle.
Heaven is a state wherein bliss and devotion mingle,
   And such was mine this morn: I could have died
Of rapture . . .

DAFYDD AP GWILYM

Easter

April 1: Easter Day

MOST glorious Lord of life, that on this day
   didst make thy triumph over death and sin:
   and having harrowed hell, didst bring away
   captivity thence captive us to win:
This joyous day, dear Lord, with joy begin,
   and grant that we for whom Thou diddest die
   being with Thy dear blood clean washed from sin,
   may live for ever in felicity.
And that Thy love we weighing worthily,
   may likewise love Thee for the same again:
   and for Thy sake that all like dear didst buy,
   with love may one another entertain.
So let us love, dear love, like as we ought,
   love is the lesson which the Lord us taught.

EDMUND SPENSER

April 2

MAKE our hearts to burn within us, O Christ, as we walk with Thee in the way and listen to Thy words; that we may go in the strength of Thy presence and Thy truth all our journey through, and at its end behold Thee, in the glory of the Eternity Trinity, God for ever and ever.

ERIC MILNER-WHITE
A Cambridge Bede Book

O Almighty God, hear Thy people who this day glorify the Resurrection of Thy Son our Lord; and guide them on from this festivity to eternal gladness, from the exulting joy of this solemnity to joys that have no end; through the same Jesus Christ our Lord.

Gothic Missal
adapted

April 3

ALMIGHTY God, who through Thine only-begotten Son Jesus Christ hast overcome death, and opened unto us the gate of everlasting life; We humbly beseech Thee that, as by Thy special grace preventing us Thou dost put into our minds good desires, so by Thy continual help we may bring the same to good effect; through the same Jesus Christ our Lord, who liveth and reigneth with Thee and the Holy Ghost, ever one God, world without end.

Book of Common Prayer

April 4

GLORY be to Thee, O Lord, glory to Thee, Creator of the light and enlightener of the world . . . O by Thy Resurrection raise us up into newness of life, supplying to us frames of repentance. The God of peace, who did bring again from the dead the great Shepherd of the sheep, through the blood of the everlasting covenant, our Lord Jesus Christ, perfect us in every good work to do His will, working in us what is acceptable before Him, through Jesus Christ, to whom be glory for ever.

LANCELOT ANDREWES
The Private Prayers of Lancelot Andrewes

April 5

BLESSED be the God and Father of our Lord Jesus Christ, who according to His abundant mercy hath begotten us again unto a lively hope by the resurrection of Jesus Christ from the dead, to an inheritance incorruptible, undefiled, and that fadeth not away, to joy and rejoicing unspeakable and full of glory in Him; to whom with Thee, O Father, and Thee, O Holy Spirit, one blessed Trinity, be ascribed all honour, might, majesty, and dominion, now and for ever.

adapted from 1 Peter

April 6

ALMIGHTY God, who didst raise from the dead our Lord Jesus Christ and didst set Him at Thy right hand in glory everlasting, I thank Thee for this hope of immortality with which through many ages Thou hast cheered and enlightened the souls of Thy saints, and which Thou didst most surely seal through the same Jesus Christ our Lord.

JOHN BAILLIE
A Diary of Private Prayer

April 7

THANKS be unto Thee, O Christ, because Thou hast broken for us the bonds of sin and brought us into fellowship with the Father;

Thanks be unto Thee, O Christ, because Thou hast overcome death and opened to us the gates of eternal life;

Thanks be unto Thee, O Christ, because where two or three are gathered together in Thy name there art Thou in the midst of them;

Thanks be unto Thee, O Christ, because Thou ever livest to make intercession for us.

For these and all other benefits of Thy mighty resurrection, thanks be unto Thee, O Christ.

New Every Morning

April 8

I ADORE and praise and bless Thee, O Lord Jesus Christ, giving thanks for the love and confidence with which, having overcome death, rising from the tomb Thou hast glorified our human flesh; and, ascending into heaven, hast placed it at the right hand of God; beseeching Thee on behalf of the souls for which I pray, that Thou wilt deign to make them partakers of Thy glory and Thy victory.

The True Prayers of St. Gertrude
and St. Mechtilde

BRIGHT, O Lord, is the Heavenly Ray; by whose unwonted light, brought to us through the Resurrection of Thy Son, the horror of the perpetual night is shattered. We bear witness to the glory of Thy mighty works; for Thou didst make the day of things that pass radiant with a Light which is eternal. Do Thou, therefore, Almighty God, Father of our Lord, receive in Thine unmoved serenity the supplications that rise to heaven from Thy praying people. Strengthen us. Grant us the gifts of hope. To them that make offering give Thou peace, and to them that are dead give the quiet of eternal rest.

Mozarabic Missal

O CHRIST, whose wondrous birth meanest nothing unless we be born again, whose death and sacrifice nothing unless we die unto sin, whose resurrection nothing if thou be risen alone: Raise and exalt us, O Saviour, both now to the estate of grace and hereafter to the state of glory; where with the Father and the Holy Spirit thou livest and reignest, God for ever and ever.

ERIC MILNER-WHITE
Cambridge Bede Book

The glory of the world

April 11

Sweet sovereign Lord of this so pined-for Spring,
How breathe the homage of but one poor heart
With such small compass of Thy everything?

Ev'n though I knew this were my life's last hour,
It yet would lie, past hope, beyond my power
One instant of my gratitude to prove,
My praise, my love.

That "Everything"!—when this, my human dust,
Whereto return I must,
Were scant to bring to bloom a single flower!

WALTER DE LA MARE
Collected Poems

April 12

But let my soul praise Thee that it may love Thee,
and let it tell Thee Thy mercies that it may praise Thee.
Without ceasing Thy whole creation speaks Thy praise—
the spirit of every man by the words that his mouth
directs to Thee, animals and lifeless matter by the mouth
of those who look upon them that so our soul rises out of
its mortal weariness unto Thee, helped upward by the
things Thou hast made and passing beyond them unto
Thee who hast wonderfully made them: and there
refreshment is and strength unfailing.

ST. AUGUSTINE
Confessions

ALL shall extol Thee, Thou Creator of all:
  O God,
Who openest every day the doors of the gates of the East,
And cleavest the windows of the firmament,
Bringing forth the sun from his place,
And the moon from her dwelling:
Giving light to the whole world and the inhabitants
    thereof,
Whom Thou createdst by the attribute of mercy.

In mercy Thou givest light to the earth
And to them that dwell thereon,
And in Thy goodness renewest the creation every day
    continually.
O King, Thou alone hast been exalted of yore;
Praised, glorified and extolled from days of old.

Jewish Prayer
Service of the Orthodox Synagogue for the
Festival of Tabernacles

CREATOR Spirit, who broodest everlastingly over the
lands and waters of earth, enduring them with forms and
colours which no human skill can copy, give me to-day,
I beseech Thee, the mind and heart to rejoice in Thy
creation.

JOHN BAILLIE
A Diary of Private Prayer

Almighty One, in the woods I am blessed. Happy everyone in the woods. Every tree speaks through Thee. O God! What glory in the woodland! On the heights is peace—peace to serve Him.

LUDWIG VAN BEETHOVEN

April 15

O Love Divine and Great,
Why dost Thou still besiege my heart?
Of me infatuate Thou art,
From me Thou canst not rest!

If I come forth by way of Light,
Love, Love is all around;
In radiance painted on the skies,
In colour on the ground:
They plead with me, in beauty drowned,
To take Thee to my breast.

If I come forth by Heaven's gate,
O what is this I hear?
What is this woven mist of sound
That breaks upon mine ear?
Here's no escape! Thy voice is clear,—
'Tis Love, in music drest.

O Love, why do I flee from Thee?
Why should I fear to yield?
Because Thou wouldst re-make my heart,
In fires of love annealed?
No more myself, in Thee concealed,
And by Thy love possessed.

Lead me to Christ, who died for me,
Draw me from sea to shore:
And make me mourn in penitence
The wounds and griefs He bore:
Why did He suffer pains so sore?
That I might be at rest.

JACOPONE DA TODI
*Part of a poem written when he came out
into the glory of the world again
after long imprisonment*

April 16

WE magnify Thee, O Lord, we bless the excellency of Thy name in the great works of Thy hands, the manifold vestures of earth and sky and sea, the course of the stars and light, the songs of birds, the hues of flowers, the frame and attributes of everything that hath breath, and, upholding all, Thy wisdom, marvellous worthy to be praised; but most, that by Thy sure promise we now do only taste the glory that shall be revealed, when Thou, O God, wilt take the power and reign, world without end.

Memorials Upon Several Occasions

I offer Thee—
Every flower that ever grew,
Every bird that ever flew,
Every wind that ever blew.
Good God!
Every thunder rolling,
Every church bell tolling,
Every leaf and sod.
Laudamus Te!
I offer Thee—
Every wave that ever moved,
Every heart that ever loved,
Thee, thy Father's Well-Beloved.
Dear Lord.
Every river dashing,
Every lightning flashing,
Like an angel's sword.
Benedicamus Te.
I offer Thee—
Every cloud that ever swept
O'er the skies, and broke and wept
In rain, and with the flowerets slept.
My King!
Each communicant praying,
Every angel staying
Before Thy throne to sing.
Adoramus Te!
I offer Thee—
Every flake of virgin snow,
Every spring of earth below,
Every human joy and woe,
My Love!

O Lord! And all Thy glorious
Self o'er death victorious,
Throned in heaven above.

Glorificamus Te!
Ancient Irish Prayer

April 18

BLESSED art Thou, O Lord, who didst create the firmament of heaven, the two lights, sun and moon, the greater and the lesser, and the stars for lights, for signs, for seasons, to rule over day and night. Blessed art Thou, O Lord, for waters above the heavens, for showers, dew, hail, snow as wool, clouds from the ends of the earth; lightnings, thunders, winds out of Thy treasures, storms; waters beneath the heavens, for drinking and for bathing. Blessed art Thou, O Lord.

LANCELOT ANDREWES
The Private Prayers of Lancelot Andrewes
adapted

April 19

PRAISE the Lord! ye heavens, adore Him;
Praise him, angels, in the height;
Sun and moon, rejoice before Him,
Praise Him, all ye stars and light:
Praise the Lord! for He hath spoken,
Worlds His mighty voice obeyed;
Laws, which never shall be broken,
For their guidance He hath made.

Hymn of the Foundling Hospital

Hosanna upon the earth . . . O Lord, vouchsafe
blessings of fountains and the deep beneath, courses of
sun, conjunctions of moons, summits of eastern mountains, of the everlasting hills.

LANCELOT ANDREWES
The Private Prayers of Lancelot Andrewes

April 20

THE kingdoms of the world, are become the kingdoms
of our Lord and of his Christ; and He shall reign for
ever and ever.

We give Thee thanks, O Lord God Almighty which
art, and wast, and art to come; because Thou hast taken
to Thee Thy great power and hast reigned.

Thou art worthy, O Lord, to receive glory and honour
and power; for Thou hast created all things, and for
Thy pleasure they are and were created.

The Book of Revelation

For our friends

April 21

LORD, Thou seest well that many there be which trust to my prayer for grace, that Thou showest to me more than I am worthy. Thou wost well Lord, that I am not such as they ween, but though my prayer be unworthy, take regard to their lowliness and to their devotion, and what they desire to Thy worship, grant them of Thy goodness. Grant them and me and to all other for whom we be holden to pray, grace to love what is to Thy liking, Thee to love to Thy most pleasing, nothing to desire that Thee should displease, all manner temptations mightily to withstand, all other vanities for Thy love to despise, Thee good Lord, ever to have in mind, and in Thy service for to abide till our life's end.

A Priest's Prayer
Bodleian MS

April 22

LORD, I see clearly that any affection which I have ever had is scarcely as one drop in the vast ocean of all the seas, when compared with the tenderness of Thy divine Heart towards those whom I love . . . Therefore I cannot even by one thought wish anything other than that which Thy almighty wisdom has appointed for each of them . . . Lord, bless Thy special friends and mine, according to the good pleasure of Thy divine goodness.

The True Prayers of St. Gertrude
and St. Mechtilde

91

April 23

TEACH us, O Father, to trust Thee with life and with
   death,
And (though this is harder by far)
With the life and the death of those that are dearer to us
   than our life.

Teach us stillness and confident peace
In Thy perfect will,
Deep calm of soul, and content
In what Thou wilt do with these lives Thou hast given.

Teach us to wait and be still,
To rest in Thyself,
To hush this clamorous anxiety,
To lay in Thine arms all this wealth Thou hast given.

Thou lovest these souls that we love
With a love as far surpassing our own
As the glory of noon surpasses the gleam of a candle.

Therefore will we be still,
And trust in Thee.

J. S. HOYLAND

O GOD, our heavenly Father, who hast commanded us to love one another as Thy children, and hast ordained the highest friendship in the bond of Thy Spirit, we beseech Thee to maintain and preserve us always in the same bond, to Thy glory, and our mutual comfort, with all those to whom we are bound by any special tie, either of nature or of choice; that we may be perfected together in that love which is from above, and which never faileth when all other things shall fail. Send down the dew of Thy heavenly grace upon us, that we may have joy in each other that passeth not away; and having lived together in love here according to Thy commandment, may live forever together with them, being made one in Thee, in Thy glorious kingdom hereafter, through Jesus Christ our Lord.

Hickes' Devotions

LORD, I beseech Thee on behalf of all who have recommended themselves to my prayers, and who cherish the memory of Thy countenance; that they may at last behold Thee. May the light of Thy countenance be their everlasting happiness. O most loving Lord, our Brother, deign to offer to the Father all the good works which they have done, but multiplied a hundredfold by Thee; and, wherever they have failed, to supply for them with Thine. And so lead their souls to Thy Heavenly Father, in the

presence of all Thy saints, enriched inestimably. Lord,
I praise Thee; in Thy eternity, in Thy immensity, in Thy
beauty, in Thy truth, in Thy justice.

The True Prayers of St. Gertrude
and St. Mechtilde
adapted

April 26

TWO GAELIC BLESSINGS

BE the great God between thy two shoulders
To protect thee in thy going and in thy coming,
Be the Son of Mary Virgin near thine heart,
And be the perfect spirit upon thee pouring—
Oh, the perfect spirit upon thee pouring!

May God shield thee,
May God fill thee,
May God watch thee.
May God bring thee
To the land of peace,
To the country of the King,
To the peace of eternity.

The Sun Dances
Prayers from the Gaelic
adapted

Most High God, our loving Father, we humbly beseech Thee for all those near and dear to us, those for whom we are bound to pray, and those for whom no-one prays. Grant them pardon for their sins, perfect their work, grant them their heart's desires, and keep them close to Thee.

Anon.

O Fountain of Love, love Thou our friends and teach them to love thee with all their hearts, that they may think and speak and do only such things as are well pleasing to Thee; through Jesus Christ our Lord.

ST. ANSELM

April 28

O Lord our God, whose might is without compare and whose glory surpasses understanding, whose mercy is without measure and love of men beyond telling; look Thou Thyself O Master, according to Thy tenderness of heart, on us and all whom we love; and deal with us, and all for whom we pray, in the riches of Thy mercies and Thy compassions.

adapted from the *Liturgy of St. John Chrysostom*

April 29

LORD, we thank Thee for all the love that has been given to us, for the love of family and friends, and above all for your love poured out upon us every moment of our lives in steadfast glory. Forgive our unworthiness. Forgive the many times we have disappointed those who love us, have failed them, wearied them, saddened them. Failing them we have failed you, and hurting them we have wounded our Saviour who for love's sake died for us. Lord, have mercy on us, and forgive. You do not fail those who love you. You do not change nor vary. Teach us your own constancy in love, your humility, selflessness and generosity. Look in pity on our small and tarnished loving, protect, foster and strengthen it, that it may be less unworthy to be offered to you and to your children. O Light of the world, teach us how to love.

April 30

A PRAYER FOR ENEMIES

MERCIFUL and loving Father,
> We beseech Thee most humbly, even with all our hearts, to pour out upon our enemies with bountiful hand, whatsoever things Thou knowest will do them good.
> And chiefly a sound and uncorrupt mind wherethrough they may know Thee and love Thee in true charity and with their whole heart, and love us, Thy children, for Thy sake.
> Let not their first hating of us turn to their harm, seeing that we cannot do them good for want of ability.

Lord, we desire their amendment and our own. Separate them not from us by punishing them, but join and knit them to us by Thy favourable dealing with them. And seeing that we be all ordained to be citizens of one everlasting City, let us begin to enter into that way here already by mutual Love which may bring us right forth thither.

Old English prayer

MAY

FOR PRISONERS

THE ASCENSION OF OUR LORD JESUS CHRIST

WHITSUNTIDE

THE HOLY TRINITY

LISTEN friends.
With drowsy eyes
I have seen
Something I want to tell you.

It is daybreak. Opposite me
a prisoner wakes up.
He raises himself on one elbow.
Takes out a cigarette. Sits up.
His gaze as he smokes
is lost,
and his forehead is untroubled.
(The wind is dreaming
in the window.)
He draws at the cigarette. Bends forward.

Takes a piece of bread,
eats it slowly
and then begins to cry.
(This does not matter perhaps.
I am just telling you.)
As for me, you know that the flagstones
have worn down the core of my heart,
but to see a man crying
is always a terrible thing.

And this prisoner is not
a broken tree. He is still unscarred.
But all at once everything he possesses
has stood before him during this quiet night . . .
With his pain in my breast
I look at him. He cannot see me.
His gaze is very distant.
He shields his eyes, crying
so softly, so deep down
that the air and the silence hardly stir.
A sudden watchword makes him start.
(In the yard
you can hear the guard changing over.)

MARCOS ANA
Written when he was a political prisoner

For prisoners

FOR POLITICAL PRISONERS

BE merciful, O Father of all mercies, to such as are
under persecution for the testimony of their conscience.

Prayer of 1585

O Lord Jesus Christ, unjustly taken prisoner and unjustly tried and condemned, we pray to you to-day for
all those men and women, all over the world, who are
in prison for their faith. From one country to another
their beliefs may differ and be at variance, but it is the
integrity of their souls that is precious in your sight, their
courage and loyalty, and these we beg you to preserve
for them in strength and purity. Comfort them, O Lord
of Compassion, in loneliness and despair, and comfort
and succour those who love them and must fend without
them. To those who have the care of them, O Lord, grant
wisdom and kindness, and that respect for a differing
faith that you asked of us with your command that we
should love our enemies. And to all of us, O Lord, the
prisoners and those who look after them, and we who
pray for them, grant the light of Thy Holy Spirit that
shall lead us into all truth.

May 2

O THOU, who hast all power in Heaven and earth; Come and let the light of Thy divine Presence illuminate the shadows of the prison-house, and fill the hearts of our brothers in bonds with hope and courage to endure patiently each his peculiar burdens and trials. Support and comfort any who are cast down, or forsaken by earthly friends, or who suffer physical or mental pain or sickness. And if any are appointed to go hence, be Thou their rod and staff through the dark valley, and at the last receive them unto Thyself in Paradise.

O. G.
A life prisoner

May 3

WE most earnestly beseech thee, O Thou Lover of mankind, to look in Thy mercy upon all prisoners. Send down into their hearts the peace of heaven. Give life to their souls and let no deadly sin prevail against them, or any of Thy people. Deliver all who are in trouble, for Thou art our God, who settest the captives free; who givest hope to the hopeless, and help to the helpless; and who art the Haven of the shipwrecked. Give Thy pity, pardon and refreshment to them, and to us who pray for them. Preserve us, in our pilgrimage through this life, from hurt and danger, and grant that we may end our lives well-pleasing to Thee and free from sin.

Adapted from the *Liturgy of St. Mark*

FOR YOUNG PRISONERS

O LORD Jesus Christ, yourself a prisoner for our sakes
and sinless in your bonds, we bring to your great love
and unending compassion all prisoners who are young,
and all who are first offenders, those who have come
where they are through misfortune or sudden temptation, and are afraid and bewildered. Lord, uphold them
in their shame and confusion, protect them from evil
and bring to their help those who will steady and
comfort them. We beseech you, O Lord, may the days
pass hopefully for them, and may they come to their
freedom again unembittered and unharmed.

May 5

FOR PRISONERS' FAMILIES

WE pray to you, O Lord, for the broken homes of prisoners, wives left without their husbands and children
fatherless, whole families in fear as they face the loneliness and hardship that lie before them. Help us, O
Lord, to help them. Show us how to bring to them all
the love and aid in our power, in whatever way is
possible for us. Bless all that is done for them, O Lord.
Comfort their fears and give them peace.

Grant your grace, O Lord, to all who have the care of prisoners, the warders and police, the prison governors, chaplains and doctors, the prison visitors, and those working for discharged prisoners. Grant to them your gifts of wisdom, courage and patience in all their difficulties. To those among them whose work is dangerous and unrewarding grant your special grace, that they may be saved from cruelty and indifference. May your love be always present with them and your mercy guide them.

May 6

FOR PRISONERS OF WAR

O MOST merciful Father, who didst send Thy Son Jesus Christ to proclaim deliverance to the captives, and to set at liberty them that are bruised: remember, we pray, all who are in captivity, prisons and bitter bondage. In loneliness cheer them, in sickness relieve them; and fill them continually with the hope of Thy everlasting mercy; through Jesus Christ our Lord.

New Every Morning

FOR PRISONERS WHO HAVE LOST HOPE

O almighty God, reveal the power of Thy grace to all who are in despair; that those who have ceased to hope may be brought, even by despair, to confide in Thee, who canst make all things new.

New Every Morning

PRAYER FOR THOSE WHO ARE TORTURED

O LORD Christ, whose death for sinners was a death of suffering, look in Thy divine compassion upon all those who, at this hour in which we pray, in prisons and in all places where there is fighting, hatred and bitterness, are enduring torment at the hands of their fellow men. All extremities of pain are known to you, Lord; may the upholding of your presence be made known to them. If they have ever heard your name, may they now remember it; if it is strange to them let them not be strangers to your courage and your peace. Lord, we know that you who know all, and love all, and have suffered all, have had each of them in your heart from all eternity; yet still we dare to pray for them, knowing that your mercy will accept our prayer and your love use it in the ways that are known to you alone.

FOR THOSE WHO INFLICT TORTURE

O LORD Christ, who prayed for those who crucified you, "Father, forgive them", look in compassion upon those who do these things, open their eyes to what they do and their hearts to your mercy. May your courage in endurance be in them the courage of refusal. And for those who command these men, those who are bound by the greater evil, we would ask that the redeeming power of your pity set them free. And grant, Lord, that we who pray for them, we who have been nurtured in your love, may not forget the sharp words and harsh thoughts that have wounded your heart as cruelly as any action of theirs. Upon us all have mercy and grant us the cleansing of penitence and the renewal of forgiveness and of love.

May 9

FOR THOSE WHO ARE CONDEMNED TO DEATH

O STRENGTH and stay, the rock of our salvation and our God, be present, we beseech you, in all prisons throughout the world where prisoners are waiting for their death. Only you, O Christ, whose own human mind endured the ordeal of knowing the exact hour and nature of a shameful death, can fully know what they suffer. May the reality and depth of your comprehending love be made known to them. For ourselves we would ask, in humble penitence, that as far as we are able in our ignorance w e may bear them company in their ordeal, uniting our love and prayer with yours that is the upholding of all men, their salvation and their peace.

Hear us, Jesus, Saviour of the world, to whom nothing is impossible; save only to be without pity for the piteous.
The True Prayers of St. Gertrude and St. Mechtilde

FOR US ALL

O SOVEREIGN Lord, Thou lover of men's lives, whose incorruptible spirit is in all things; We bring to Thee ourselves, our sins and failures, as to a merciful Father, who understandest all, and forgivest all; for Thy mercy's sake.

Ecclesiasticus
adapted by G. W. BRIGGS

O Lord forgive
　the evils men have done
　and do to-day to other men
　to wound Thee in the least of them Thy brethren.
O Lord forgive
　the pride of self that would make man supreme,
　the ruler of his universe, defying God.

My Lord, my God, my Saviour, and my King,
　I have not ought to say,
　nor any man can say, except
　　O Lord forgive.

GILBERT SHAW
The Face of Love

May 11

O Risen Saviour, bid me rise with Thee
  and seek those things which are above;
  not only seek, but set my whole heart upon them.

Thou art in heaven, ever raising lives to Thyself;
  O, by Thy grace, may mine be making that ascent
    not in dreams, but in truth,
    now, to-morrow, always.

Daily in spirit, in Thy Holy Spirit,
  Let me behold Thee on the throne of God,
    Thou King reigning in holiness,
    Thou Conqueror of all evil,
    Thou Majesty of love,
    very God and very Man,
  of glory unimaginable and eternal,
    in whom all hope is sure.

ERIC MILNER-WHITE
My God my Glory

WHO shall speak of Thy power, O Lord, and who shall be able to tell the tale of all Thy praises? Thou didst descend to human things, not leaving behind heavenly things. Thou art returned to things above, not abandoning things below. Everywhere Thou art Thy whole self, everywhere wonderful. In the flesh, Thou hast yet thy being in the Father; in thine Ascension Thou art not torn away from Thy being in man. Look upon the prayer of Thy people, holy Lord, merciful God; that in this day of Thy holy Ascension, even as glory is given to Thee on high, so grace may be vouchsafed to us below.

Mozarabic Missal

May 13

ALMIGHTY God, whose blessed Son our Saviour Jesus Christ ascended far above all heavens, that He might fill all things: Mercifully give us faith to perceive that according to His promise He abideth with His Church on earth, even unto the end of the world; through the same Jesus Christ our Lord.

Book of Common Prayer
Episcopal Church of Scotland

May 14

O Thou who, for our sakes, wast lifted up on the cross, lifted up from the grave, lifted up into glory; draw us unto Thee, O good Lord, with cords of a man, with bands of love, that we may seek Thee in prayer, may follow Thee in holy obedience, and may set our affections on things above where Thou sittest on the right hand of God.

Anon.

May 15

Lord Jesus! with what sweetness and delights,
Sure holy hopes, high joys and quick'ning flights
Dost Thou feed thine! O Thou! the hand that lifts
To Him, who gives all good and perfect gifts.
Thy glorious, bright Ascension (though remov'd
So many ages from me) is so prov'd
And by thy spirit seal'd to me, that I
Feel me a sharer in Thy victory.
     I soar and rise
     Up to the skies,
      Leaving the world their day,
    And in my flight,
    For the true light
    Go seeking all the way.

HENRY VAUGHAN

HOLY God, holy and mighty, holy living and
    immortal,
  Who didst rise from the dead on the third
    day
And didst ascend with glory into heaven
    and sit down at the right hand of the
    Father,
And shalt come again with glory to judge
    the quick and the dead,
  Have mercy upon us, O Lord.
Liturgy of the Abyssinian Jacobites

May 17

ALMIGHTY and everlasting God, so lead us into the
fellowship of heavenly joys that, born again in the Holy
Spirit, we may enter into Thy Kingdom; and that the
simple sheep may come thither, whither the noble
Shepherd has gone before.

Gregorian Sacramentary

O God who in the burning fire of Thy love wast
pleased to pour out the Holy Spirit on Thy disciples:
Grant us by the same Spirit to be new lit with heavenly
desires and with the power to fulfil them; through Jesus
Christ our Lord.

Gelasian Sacramentary

O GOD the Holy Ghost who art Light
    unto Thine elect,
  Evermore enlighten us.
Thou who art Fire of Love,
  Evermore enkindle us.
Thou who art Lord and Giver of Life,
  Evermore live in us.
Thou who bestowest sevenfold grace,
  Evermore replenish us.
As the wind is Thy symbol.
  So forward our goings.
As the dove,
  So launch us heavenwards.
As water,
  So purify our spirits.
As a cloud,
  So abate our temptations.
As dew,
  So revive our languor.
As fire,
  So purge out our dross.

CHRISTINA ROSSETTI

May 19

HEAVENLY King, Paraclete, Spirit of Truth, present in all places and filling all things, Treasury of good and Choir-master of life: come and dwell within us, cleanse us from all stains and save our souls.

Liturgy of St. John Chrysostom

Oh come, Thou refreshment of them that languish and faint. Come, Thou Star and Guide of them that sail in the tempestuous sea of the world; Thou only Haven of the tossed and shipwrecked. Come, Thou Glory and Crown of the living, and only Safeguard of the dying. Come, Holy Spirit, in much mercy, and make me fit to receive Thee.

ST. AUGUSTINE

May 20

O KING, enthroned on high,
Thou Comforter divine,
Blest Spirit of all truth, be nigh
And make us Thine.

Thou art the Source of life,
Thou art our treasure-store;
Give us Thy peace, and end our strife
For evermore.

Descend, O heavenly Dove,
Abide with us alway;
And in the fullness of Thy love
Cleanse us, we pray.

8th-century prayer

May 21

MAY thy servants, O God, be set on fire with Thy Spirit, strengthened by Thy power, illuminated by Thy splendour, filled with Thy grace, and go forward by Thine aid; and after having manfully finished our course, may we be enabled happily to enter into Thy kingdom.

Gallican Sacramentary

May 22

O HOLY Spirit of God,
   who with Thy holy breath doth cleanse the
     hearts and minds of men,
comforting them when they be in sorrow,
leading them when they be out of the way,
kindling them when they be cold,
knitting them together when they be at variance,
   and enriching them with manifold gifts;
     by whose working all things live:
We beseech Thee to maintain and daily to increase
   the gifts which Thou hast vouchsafed to us;
that with Thy light before us and within us
   we may pass through this world
     without stumbling and without straying;
who livest and reignest with the Father and the Son,
   everlastingly.

ERASMUS
A Booke of Christian Prayer

May 23

LET our souls, we beseech Thee, Almighty God, achieve this their desire, to be kindled by Thy Spirit; that being filled as lamps by Thy divine gift, we may shine like blazing lights before the presence of Thy Son Christ at his coming.

Gelasian Sacramentary

Grant, Eternal Spirit, to us who kneel before Thy darkness that it may become light by Thy grace, for we have but a sickly spark within us. Blow upon us with Thy breath, though we feel it not; lead us, though we follow not, receive us though our pride reject Thy consolation; for save by Thee we cannot come to Thee, and, unless Thou showest it, there is no end.

Anon.

May 24

IN the hour of my distress,
When temptations me oppress,
And when I my sins confess.
 Sweet Spirit comfort me!

When I lie within my bed,
Sick in heart, and sick in head,
And with doubts discomforted,
 Sweet Spirit comfort me!

When the house doth sigh and weep,
And the world is drown'd in sleep,
Yet mine eyes the watch do keep;
 Sweet Spirit comfort me!

When (God knows) I'm tossed about,
Either with despair, or doubt;
Yet before the glass be out,
   Sweet Spirit comfort me!

When the judgement is reveal'd,
And that open'd which was seal'd,
When to Thee I have appeal'd;
   Sweet Spirit comfort me!

ROBERT HERRICK

May 25

O Come, O Holy Spirit, come!
Come as holy fire and burn in us,
Come as holy wind and cleanse us,
Come as holy light and lead us,
Come as holy truth and teach us,
Come as holy forgiveness and free us,
Come as holy love and enfold us,
Come as holy power and enable us,
Come as holy life and dwell in us.
Convict us, convert us,
Consecrate us, until we are wholly Thine
   for Thy using, through Jesus Christ our Lord.

Adapted by CHARLES FRANCIS WHISTON
from an ancient prayer

May 26

O Lᴏʀᴅ Almighty, Father unbegotten, upon us miserable sinners,
Have mercy.

O Lord, who hast redeemed the work of Thy hands by
Thine only Son,
Have mercy upon us.

O Lord, Adonai, blot out our offences, and upon Thy
people
Have mercy.

O Christ, Brightness of the Father's glory, and the
express image of His person,
Have mercy upon us.

O Christ, who didst save the world at the command of
the Father,
Have mercy upon us.

O Christ, Saviour of men, eternal Life of Angels,
Have mercy upon us.

O Lord, Spirit, the Comforter, Dispenser of pardon,
Have mercy upon us.

O Lord, Fountain of mercy and of sevenfold grace,
Have mercy upon us.

O Lord, most pitiful Forgiver, proceeding from Both,

O most bountiful Giver of gifts, Teacher, Quickener, of
Thy goodness
Have mercy upon us.

Litany from the *Sarum Missal*

ALMIGHTY and everlasting God, who hast given unto
us Thy servants grace, by the confession of a true faith,
to acknowledge the glory of the eternal Trinity, and in
the power of the Divine Majesty to worship the Unity;
We beseech Thee that Thou wouldest keep us steadfast
in this faith, and evermore defend us from all adversities,
who livest and reignest, one God, world without end.

Book of Common Prayer

PRAYER TO THE HOLY TRINITY

I am bending my knee
In the eye of the Father who created me,
In the eye of the Son who purchased me,
In the eye of the Spirit who cleansed me,
    In friendship and affection.
Through Thine own Anointed One, O God,
Bestow upon us fullness in our need,
        Love towards God,
        The affection of God,
        The smile of God,
        The wisdom of God,
        The grace of God,
        The fear of God,
        And the will of God,

To do on the world of the Three,
As angels and saints
Do in heaven;
　　Each shade and light,
　　Each day and night,
　　Each time in kindness,
　　Give Thou us Thy Spirit.

The Sun Dances
Prayers from the Gaelic

May 29

GIVE us, O Lord God, a deep sense of Thy holiness; how Thou art of purer eyes than to behold iniquity, and canst not overlook or pass by that which is evil.

Give us no less, O Lord, a deep sense of Thy wonderful love towards us; how Thou wouldst not let us alone in our ruin, but didst come after us, in the Person of Thy Son Jesus Christ to bring us back to our true home with Thee.

Quicken in us, O Lord, the Spirit of gratitude, of loyalty and of sacrifice, that we may seek in all things to please Him who humbled Himself for us, even to the death of the Cross, by dying unto sin and living unto righteousness; through the same Jesus Christ our Lord.

DEAN VAUGHAN

May 30

FATHER most holy, merciful and tender;
Jesus our Saviour, with the Father reigning;
Spirit of mercy, Advocate, Defender,
Light never waning.

Trinity sacred, Unity unshaken;
Deity perfect, giving and forgiving,
Light of the Angels, Life of the forsaken,
Hope of all living.

Maker of all things, all thy creatures praise Thee;
Lo, all things serve Thee through Thy whole creation:
Hear us, Almighty, hear us as we raise Thee
Heart's adoration.

To the almighty triune God be glory:
Highest and greatest, help Thou our endeavour;
We too would praise Thee, giving honour worthy,
Now and for ever.

10th-century prayer
translated by PERCY DEARMER

May 31

To God the Father, who first loved us and made us
accepted in the Beloved; to God the Son, who loved us,
and washed us from our sins in His own blood; to God
the Holy Ghost, who sheds the love of God abroad in
our hearts, be all love and all glory, for time and for
eternity.

BISHOP THOMAS KEN

Blessing and honour and thanksgiving and praise more
than we can utter, more than we can conceive, be unto
Thee, O holy and glorious Trinity, Father, Son, and
Holy Ghost, by all angels, all men, all creatures, for ever
and ever.

BISHOP THOMAS KEN

JUNE

FOR THE POOR AND HOMELESS,
THE REFUGEES, THE LONELY,
THE UNEMPLOYED

THE SACRAMENT OF HOLY COMMUNION

FOR PEACE

HELP, GOOD SHEPHERD

TURN not aside, Shepherd, to see
How bright the constellations are,
Hanging in heaven, or on the tree;
The skyborn or terrestrial star

Brood not upon; the waters fleet,
Willows, or Thy crown-destined thorn,
Full of her rubies, as is meet,
Or whitening in the eye of morn,

Pause not beside: Shepherds' delight,
The pipe and tabor in the vale,
And mirthful watchfires of a night,
And herdsman's rest in wattled pale,

Forsake, though deeply earned: and still
Sound with Thy crook the darkling flood,
Still range the sides of shelvy hill
And call about in underwood:

For on the hill are many strayed,
Some held in thickets plunge and cry,
And the deep waters make us afraid.
Come then and help us, or we die.

RUTH PITTER
Urania

**For the poor, the homeless,
the refugees, the lonely,
the unemployed**

June 1

THOU who didst spread Thy creating arms to the stars,
strengthen our arms with power to intercede when we
lift up our hands unto thee.

Armenian Liturgy

Here is Thy footstool and there rest Thy feet where
    live the poorest, the lowliest, and lost.
When I try to bow to Thee, my obeisance cannot reach
    down to the depth where Thy feet rest among the
    poorest, and lowliest, and lost.
Pride can never approach to where Thou walkest in the
    clothes of the humble among the poorest, and
    lowliest, and lost.
My heart can never find its way to where Thou keepest
    company with the companionless among the
    poorest, the lowliest, and the lost.

RABINDRANATH TAGORE
Gitanjali, No. X

June 2

O GOD, the Father of the forsaken, the Help of the weak, the Supplier of the needy, who teachest us that love towards the race of man is the bond of perfectness, and the imitation of Thy blessed self; open our eyes and touch our hearts, that we may see and do, both for this world and for that which is to come, the things which belong unto our peace. Pour into us a spirit of humility; let nothing be done but in devout obedience to Thy will, thankfulness for Thine unspeakable mercies, and love to Thy beloved Son Christ Jesus.

ANTHONY ASHLEY COOPER,
EARL OF SHAFTESBURY
adapted

June 3

JESUS, Son of man, look in mercy upon all who suffer the lack of livelihood and, like Thee, have not where to lay their head: let Thy pity and compassion move us to house the homeless and lighten the burdens of the needy and distressed: that in Thee all the families of the earth may be blessed.

O Lord Jesus Christ, born in a stable: hear the cry of the homeless and refugees; and so move our wills by Thy Spirit that we cease not until all have found home and livelihood, for Thy name's sake.

FREDERICK B. MACNUTT

June 4

LORD Jesus, who as a child didst flee with Thy family to a strange country, look with pity we beseech Thee upon the refugees scattered throughout the world, victims of war and persecution, tyranny and oppression. Save them from despair, heal their bitterness, give them hope. And as they have suffered at the hands of their fellow men, so may we, their fellow men, never forget their needs; and may the causes for their homelessness be rooted out of our world. In Thy Name we ask it.

HENDERIKA J. RYNBERGEN
adapted

June 5

ALMIGHTY God, King of Kings, who hast called us into a Kingdom not of this world; send forth, we pray, Thy spirit unto the dark habitations of guilt and woe. Reach the heart of every oppression, and make arrogancy dumb before Thee. Still the noise of our strife and the tumult of the people. Put to shame the false idols of every heart. Carry faith to the doubting, hope to the fearful, strength to the weak, comfort to all who mourn. Commit Thy word, O Lord, to faithful witnesses, that Thy Kingdom may speedily come and Thy will be done on earth as it is in heaven.

JOHN HEUSS

June 6

O GOD our Saviour, we thank you for your great love that chose always to suffer alone that all our solitudes should bring with them the companionship of your understanding. We thank you and remember with reverence and love your loneliness in temptation, the loneliness of the misunderstanding you endured, your lonely agony in the garden, your loneliness when you stood before your judges, denied and forsaken by your friends, your loneliness upon the cross, believing yourself forsaken even of God, your loneliness in death and in the tomb. We thank you and love you and remember in our love all who suffer the pains of loneliness, those who are lonely in crippling infirmities of mind and body, the old and those who are bereaved, those who feel themselves friendless and forsaken, those lonely in unemployment, poverty, captivity or exile. We pray for them, O Lord, that as you carry them in your heart of compassion so they may find you at the heart of their loneliness, and in their finding know the joy of your Presence.

June 7

O LORD, our heavenly Father, we commend to Thy protecting care and compassion the men and women of this and every land now suffering distress and anxiety through lack of work: prosper, we pray Thee, the councils of those who are engaged in the ordering of industrial life, that all people may be set free from want and fear, and may be enabled to work in security and peace, for the happiness of the common life and the well-being of their countries. Through Jesus Christ our Lord.

Anon.

June 8

O CHRIST, who camest not to be ministered unto but to minister, have mercy upon all who labour faithfully to serve the common good. O Christ, who didst feed the hungry multitude with loaves and fishes, have mercy upon all who labour to earn their daily bread. O Christ, who didst call unto Thyself all them that labour and are heavy laden, have mercy upon all whose work is beyond their strength. And to Thee, with the Father and the Holy Spirit, be all the glory and the praise.

JOHN BAILLIE
A Diary of Private Prayer

June 9

THOU, O Lord, providest enough for all men with Thy most liberal and bountiful hand; but whereas Thy gifts are, in respect of Thy goodness and free favour, made common to all men, we (through our naughtiness, niggardship, and distrust) do make them private and peculiar. Correct Thou the thing which our iniquity hath put out of order; let Thy goodness supply that which our niggardliness hath plucked away. Give Thou meat to the hungry and drink to the thirsty; comfort Thou the sorrowful; cheer up the dismayed; strengthen Thou the weak; deliver Thou them that are prisoners; and give Thou hope and courage to them that are out of heart.

Anon.

June 10

MERCIFUL Father, we come to Thee confessing the sins of our civilization, in which we have all shared. We have been so bent upon our selfish ends that we would not stop to have mercy. When we have seen those whom the injustices of the world have bruised and beaten, we have passed by on the other side. We have built around ourselves the walls of privilege, within which we might not hear the passion of exploited men, the weeping of women, the bitter cry of children robbed of happy youth. O God of judgement, make us fit to ask for Thy forgiveness, before it is too late.

Anon.

June 11

FOR THE CONGREGATION

VOUCHSAFE to look down on those who here pray with Thine humble servant, and on those who are absent. Remember, O Lord, my littleness; not the faults and ignorance of the past, but according to Thy mercies, for if Thou take count of our iniquities, who shall abide it? Thy mercy is upon us. Come to me, cleanse me and let Thy grace abound. Remember, O Lord, those whom we remember and those whom we forget. Accept in heaven their prayers and make them worthy of Thy presence and Thy help. Strengthen them by Thy might, instruct them by Thy changelessness; for Thou, O God, art our protector.

West Syrian Liturgy

June 12

THEE do I supplicate, God, in whom is all harmony, all illumination, all steadfastness, all abundance and all life! God, who givest us the Bread of Life, help me to love Thee alone, Thee alone follow, Thee alone seek, Thee alone serve. Command, I pray, and I hope that I shall do all things which Thou commandest.

ST. AUGUSTINE
adapted

June 13

STAINED though I be with the multitude of sins, reject me not, our master, our Lord, and our God! For lo! not as though I were worthy have I drawn near to this, Thy divine and heavenly mystery; but looking up to Thy goodness, I raise my cry to Thee—God, be merciful to me a sinner!

Liturgy of St. James

June 14

> FROM unclean lips,
> From an evil heart,
> From an impure tongue,
> Out of a soul defiled,
> Receive, O Christ, my prayer.
> All my sins take from me, O God of all;
> That with a clean heart,
> With a trembling mind,
> And a contrite spirit,
> I may partake of Thy pure
> And all-holy Mysteries.
> My Master and my God,
> Whosoever partaketh of Thy divine
> And hallowing grace,
> Assuredly, never is alone
> But is with Thee, O Christ,
> The thrice-glorious Light
> Which lighteth the world.

SIMEON THE NEW THEOLOGIAN
adapted

LET all mortal flesh keep silence, and stand in fear and trembling, and ponder nothing earthly-minded; for the King of Kings, the Lord of Lords, Christ our God, cometh to be sacrificed, to give Himself as food to the faithful. Before Him go the Choir of angels, Powers and Dominations, the many-eyed Cherubim and six-winged Seraphim, covering their faces and crying aloud, Alleluia! Alleluia! Alleluia!

Liturgy of St. James

MY Lord, my King,
    my love goes out to Thee,
    drawn by the love
    wherewith I am enabled to return Thy love.
Lamb of God, slain from the first beginning of all time,
Lamb of God, slain until the consummation of the end,
Lamb of God, slain upon a day in history,
    throned in death
    upon the altar of Thy Cross,
    the one and only sacrifice for sin,
        we magnify Thy Name.

GILBERT SHAW
The Face of Love

THE CONSECRATION

This is my Lord,
    beside and about me,
        coming and entering and abiding within.
This is my Lord, to whom I belong:
This, my Lord, calling me nearer and nearer.

This is my Lord, who died for me:
This, my Lord, who taketh away my sin:
This, my Lord, clothing me in his righteousness:
This, my Lord, giving strength for to-day and to-morrow:
This, my Lord, with His own hands feeding me
        with His own life,
        with His Body and His Blood,
        with His heart and His soul.

As He would dwell in me,
    may I dwell in Him
        for ever and ever.

ERIC MILNER-WHITE
My God my Glory

June 18

WE thank Thee, our Father, for the life and knowledge which Thou hast made known unto us through Jesus Thy Servant. To Thee be glory for ever. As this broken bread, once scattered upon the mountains, has been gathered together and been made one, so may Thy Church be gathered together from the ends of the earth into Thy Kingdom; for Thine is the glory and the power through Jesus Christ for ever.

Didache
2nd century

June 19

WE yield Thee hearty thanks, O Lord Jesus Christ, for Thine unutterable love in vouchsafing to redeem mankind by Thine own death; and we beseech Thee, suffer not Thy blood to have been shed in vain for us; that we, growing up in Thee by continual increase of heavenly strength, may become fit members of Thy mystical body, which is the Church, and never swerve from that most holy Covenant which Thou madest with Thy chosen disciples in the last supper, by distributing the bread unto them, and by reaching them the cup; and through them with all those who through baptism are grateful unto Thy company.

ERASMUS
A Booke of Christian Prayer
adapted

FOR THE CONGREGATION

STRENGTHEN, O our Lord, the hands that have been stretched out and have received the holy thing for the pardon of offences.

Account them worthy every day to yield fruits to Thy Godhead.

The mouths which have praised Thee within the holy place,

Do Thou account worthy to sing praise.

The ears which have heard the voice of Thy praises,

Let Thou not, O my Lord, hear the voice of alarm,

The eyes that have seen Thy great compassion,

Again, O my Lord, let them see Thy blessed hope.

The tongues, also, that have cried Holy,

Do Thou dispose to speak truth.

The feet that walk within the church,

Make them to walk within the land of light.

Our congregation which hath worshipped Thy Godhead,

Multiply towards it every help.

Liturgy of Malabar

For peace

LITANY OF PEACE

In peace let us beseech the Lord
for the peace that is from above
    and the salvation of our souls;
for the peace of the whole world
    and the holy churches of God
    and of all men;
for our homes, that they may be holy,
    and for all our pastors, teachers and governors;
for our city [township, village] and country
    and all who dwell therein;
for all that travel by land, by air, by water;
for the sick and all who need Thy pity and
    protection.
On all, have mercy, and preserve all, O God,
    by Thy grace:
for unto Thee, O Lord, is due glory, honour,
    and worship
        world without end.

    Adapted from the *Liturgy of St. John Chrysostom*

June 22

LORD give us peace in our days, for there is none that
fighteth for us but Thou alone our God.
Lord, peace be made in Thy strength
And plenty in Thy towers.

God, of whom be holy desires, rightful counsels and
just deeds, give to Thy servants that peace that the world
may not give, so that our hearts may be given to keep
Thine hests and dread of our enemies may be taken from
us, so that our times may be peaceable by Thy protection, by our Lord Jesus Christ Thy Son, that liveth with
Thee and reigneth God, by all worlds of worlds.

MS Douce

June 23

JESUS, Saviour of human activity to which You have
given meaning, Saviour of human suffering to which You
have given living value, be also the Saviour of human
unity; compel us to discard our pettinesses, and to
venture forth, resting upon You, into the undaunted
ocean of charity.

PIERRE TEILHARD DE CHARDIN
Le Milieu Divin

FOR RACIAL PEACE

O GOD, who makest man to be of one mind in an house and hast called us into the fellowship of Thy dear Son: draw into closer unity, we beseech Thee, the people of all races in this and every land; that in fellowship with Thee they may understand and help one another, and that, serving Thee, they may find their perfect freedom; through the same Thy Son Jesus Christ our Lord.

JOOST DE BLANK

God bless Africa
Guard her children
Guide her leaders
Grant her peace
In Jesus Christ's Name.

TREVOR HUDDLESTON

June 25

O Lord, forgive the cruelties of men in every age,
   their insensibility to others' pain,
   the deliberation which gives pain
      to satisfy and to express
   the evil that rebels from love's surrender to others'
         needs
      to exalt itself.

O Lord, forgive the carelessness that passes by,
   the blunted consciences that will not see,
      or fear to see,
   the wrongs men do to other men.

Most merciful, most loving Judge, Redeemer of mankind,
   Thou dost restore the fallen,
   Thou dost seek out the scattered sheep.

GILBERT SHAW
The Face of Love

June 26

O God, by whose power alone men are enabled to live
together as brethren; Look upon the broken body of our
humanity, and grant that wherever men meet in council
for the ordering of the world, Thy Holy Spirit may
bring them into unity. Let Thy forgiveness make us
ready to forgive and to be reconciled to those from whom
we are estranged; through Jesus Christ our Lord.

New Every Morning

WE pray for all mankind.
Though divided into nations and races,
Yet are all men Thy children,
Drawing from Thee their life and being,
Commanded by Thee to obey Thy laws,
Each in accordance with the power to know and
    understand them.

Cause hatred and strife to vanish,
That abiding peace may fill the earth,
And humanity may everywhere be blessed with the
    fruits of peace.
So shall the spirit of brotherhood among men
Show forth their faith that
      Thou art the Father of all.

Jewish Prayer
Liberal Jewish Prayer Book

June 28

O GOD, who wouldst fold both heaven and earth in a
single peace; Let the design of Thy great love lighten
upon the waste of our wraths and sorrows and give peace
to Thy Church, peace among nations, peace in our
dwellings, and peace in our hearts; through Thy Son,
our Saviour, Jesus Christ.

ERIC MILNER-WHITE
Memorials Upon Several Occasions

June 29

O CHRIST, the peace of the things that are on high, and the great rest of those that are below, establish O Lord in Thy peace and rest the four regions of the world. Destroy wars and battles from the ends of the earth, and disperse all those that delight in war; and by Thy divine mercy pacify the Church and the Kingdom, that we may have a safe habitation in all soberness and piety. And through Thy mercy and love forgive the debts and sins of them that are departed this life.

Liturgy of Malabar

June 30

ETERNAL God, in whose perfect kingdom no sword is drawn but the sword of righteousness, and no strength known but the strength of love: We pray Thee so mightily to shed and spread abroad Thy Spirit, that all peoples and ranks may be gathered under one banner, of the Prince of Peace; as children of one God and Father of All; to whom be dominion and glory now and for ever.

ERIC MILNER-WHITE
Memorials Upon Several Occasions

~~~~~~

JULY
~~~~~~

FOR DELIVERANCE FROM SELF

FOR QUEEN AND COMMONWEALTH.
SCHOOLS AND UNIVERSITIES.
TEACHERS, SCIENTISTS, WRITERS,
ARTISTS, CRAFTSMEN AND FARMERS

MORNING PRAYERS

GOD strengthen me to bear myself;
That heaviest weight of all to bear,
Inalienable weight of care . . .

If I could once lay down myself,
And start self-purged upon the race
That all must run! Death runs apace.

If I could set aside myself,
And start with lightened heart upon
The road by all men overgone!

God harden me against myself,
This coward with pathetic voice
Who craves for ease, and rest and joys:

Myself, arch-traitor to myself,
My hollowest friend, my deadliest foe
My clog whatever road I go.

Yet One there is can curb myself,
Can roll the strangling load from me,
Break off the yoke and set me free.

CHRISTINA ROSSETTI

For deliverance from self

O LORD God, be Thou to me a God, and beside Thee none else, none else, naught else, with Thee.

LANCELOT ANDREWES
The Private Prayers of Lancelot Andrewes

Jesus, grant me the grace to fix my mind on Thee, especially in time of prayer, when I directly converse with Thee. Stop the motions of my wandering head, and the desires of my unstable heart, and my many vain imaginings. O beloved of my soul, take up all my thoughts here, that mine eyes, abstaining from all vain and hurtful sights, may become worthy to behold Thee face to face in Thy glory for ever.

From the *Jesus Psalter*

My Lord, and Master of my life,
    grant me Thy grace and living Presence
      in my soul
    that Thou may'st draw me into Thyself,
    my mind renewed, transformed,
      grace by grace,
    into the new and perfect temple of Thyself,
    through suffering cleansed, through suffering made
      one life with Thee
      to glorify Thy Name.

Lead Thou me forth from out the city of myself,
   upon the way to be for ever one with Thee.
Give me the measure of Thy grace
   which is sufficient unto me
   at every stage upon the road,
that I may know Thee as Thou art
   my Love, my all.

GILBERT SHAW
The Face of Love

July 3

LORD, bestow on me two gifts,
   —to forget myself,
   —never to forget Thee.

Keep me from self-love, self-pity, self-will,
   in every guise and disguise,
nor ever let me measure myself by myself.
Save me from self,
   my tempter, seducer, jailor;
   corrupting desire at the spring,
   closing the avenues of grace,
   leading me down the streets of death.

Rather, let my soul devote to Thee
   its aspirations, affections, resolutions;
let my mind look unto Thee
   in all its searchings, strivings, certitudes;
let my body work for Thee
   with its full health and abilities.

Let Thy love pass
    into the depth of my heart,
    into the heart of my prayer,
    into the prayer of my whole being;
so that I desert myself
    and dwell and move in Thee.
        in peace, now and evermore.

ERIC MILNER-WHITE
My God my Glory

July 4

I ADORE Thee, Lord Jesus, dwelling in my heart. I beseech Thee abide in me, in all the tranquillity of Thy power, in all the perfection of Thy ways, in all the brightness of Thy presence and in all the holiness of Thy Spirit; that I may know the breadth and length and depth and height of Thy love: and do Thou trample down in me all power of evil in the might of Thy Spirit to the glory of God the Father.

PÈRE OLIER
adapted

July 5

LORD give us grace
  to hold to Thee
when all is weariness and fear
and sin abounds within, without,
when that which I would do I cannot do
and that I do I would not do,
when love itself is tested by the doubt
that love is false, or dead within the soul,
when every act brings new confusion, new distress,
    new opportunities, new misunderstandings,
and every thought new accusation.

Lord give us grace
  that we may know that in the darkness pressing round
  it is the mist of sin that hides Thy face
  that Thou are there
  and Thou dost know we love Thee still . . .

GILBERT SHAW
The Face of Love

July 6

O LIFE of Jesus Christ!
Mirror of Verity!
Mine own deformity
  I see in that clear Light.
Lord, thou hast shown me now,
In Thy fair holiness,
Mine utter nothingness;
  Yea, less than nothing I!

JACAPONE DA TODI

148

O God, who hast called us to open our hand, and Thou wouldest fill it, and we would not: open Thou not only our hand, but our heart also; that we may know nothing but Thee, count all things lost in comparison of Thee, and endeavour to be made like unto Thee; through Jesus Christ our Lord.

JEREMY TAYLOR

July 7

O LORD Christ, lifted on the cross that you may draw all men unto you, have mercy upon us. It is our self-love that crucified you then, and crucifies you now in every thought that turns in upon self, passing you by, in every word and deed that pierces and thrusts for self, wounding you in your children. Longing for you we yet stand far off upon the hill of Calvary, mourning for what we are, afraid of the darkness we have brought about us by what we do, clinging still to the secret sweetness of self-love, and unable to bring it to the love that burns for us upon the cross that it may die there in the flame. Lord, strengthen our weak longing for you with the great strength of your longing for us, and bring us through the darkness to where you are. Give us courage for the dying, courage for the grave, courage for the new-born love created after the pattern of your own. In our dying, Lord, in our resurrection, you will be close to us. We shall no longer be far off.

July 8

O SAVIOUR, pour upon me Thy Spirit of meekness and love, annihilate the Selfhood in me, be Thou all my life. Guide Thou my hand which trembles exceedingly upon the rock of ages.

WILLIAM BLAKE

Give us grace, O Eternal Father, that we strive to keep the way of the Cross, and carry in our hearts the image of Jesus crucified. Make us glad to conform ourselves to Thy divine will, that, being fashioned after His life-giving death, we may die according to the flesh, and live according to the Spirit of Righteousness, through the same Jesus Christ our Lord and only Saviour.

Greek Church

July 9

KEEP me, O Lord, for I am Thine by creation; guide me, for I am Thine by purchase; Thou hast redeemed me by the blood of Thy Son, and loved me with the love of a father, for I am Thy child . . . Let no hope or fear, no pleasure or pain, no accident without, no weakness within, hinder or discompose my duty, or turn me from the ways of Thy commandments. O let Thy Spirit dwell with me for ever, and make my soul just and charitable, full of honesty, full of religion, resolute and constant in holy purposes, but inflexible to evil. Make me humble and obedient, peaceable and pious; let me never envy any man's good, nor deserve to be despised myself: and if I be, teach me to bear it with meekness and charity

JEREMY TAYLOR

O MOST merciful Father, save us from ourselves, and show us the pattern of a world made new, wherein Thy will is done and all men are accepted as brothers; through Jesus Christ our Lord.

Anon.

O timeless and eternal Spirit, liberate us from the prison house of selfish desire, of worldly standards and of petty ambition into the spacious heaven of Thy love. May the peace of the eternal Father brood over us; may love of the eternal Son surround us; may the strength of the eternal Spirit dwell within us.

Anon.

For Queen and Commonwealth
Schools and universities
Teachers, scientists, writers,
artists, craftsmen and farmers

July 11

PRAYER FOR QUEEN ELIZABETH II

WE render unto Thee, O merciful and heavenly Father, most humble and hearty thanks for Thy manifold mercies so abundantly bestowed upon our Queen, unto this present hour. Continue, we beseech Thee, this Thy favourable goodness towards her; keep her in Thy faith, fear and love, that she may never fall away from Thee, but continue in Thy service all the days of her life.

Adapted from a prayer composed by
QUEEN ELIZABETH I

July 12

FOR THE QUEEN AND HER COUNSELLORS

MAY the supreme King of kings in his mercy preserve the Queen in life, guard her and deliver her from all trouble and sorrow. May He put a spirit of wisdom and understanding into her heart and into the hearts of all her counsellors, that they may uphold the peace of the realm, advance the welfare of the nation, and deal kindly and truly with all Israel. In her days and in ours, may our Heavenly Father spread the protection of peace over all the dwellers on earth; and may the Redeemer come unto Zion; and let us say, Amen.

Jewish Prayer
Authorized Daily Prayer Book

FOR THE COMMONWEALTH

LORD, bless this Kingdom and Commonwealth, that religion and virtue may season all sorts of men; that there may be peace within its gates and prosperity in all its borders. In peace so preserve it that it corrupt not; in trouble so defend it that it suffer not; and so order it, whether in plenty or in want, that it may patiently and peaceably seek Thee, the only full supply and sure foundation both of men and states, that so it may continue a place and people to do Thee service to the end of time; through Jesus Christ our only Saviour and Redeemer.

ARCHBISHOP WILLIAM LAUD

July 14

FOR OUR COUNTRY

O GOD, the God of all righteousness, mercy, and love: Give us all grace and strength to conceive and execute whatever be for Thine honour and the welfare of the nation: that we may become at last, through the merits and intercession of our Common Redeemer, a great and a happy, because a wise and understanding people; to Thy honour and glory.

LORD SALISBURY

July 15

O GOD, who dost begin and sustain all progress up to Thee in Thy kingdom: Bless our Universities and Schools, that they may convey to Thy children Thy best gifts of truth and godliness; and prepare them for the perfect citizenship alike of earth and heaven; through Jesus Christ our Lord.

ERIC MILNER-WHITE
Cambridge Bede Book

O Lord Jesus Christ, we pray Thee to pour Thy Spirit upon the students of all nations; that they may consecrate themselves to Thy service, and may come to love and understand one another through their common obedience to Thee.

Anon.

July 16

FOR TEACHERS

LORD Jesus Christ, who didst show on this earth Thy love for children: guide, we pray Thee, with Thy Spirit, those who are called to the ministry of teaching in this land; that nothing may hinder our children from growing in faith and love towards Thee, and that Thy name may be honoured both in our schools and in our homes.

New Every Morning

Lord Jesus, merciful and patient, grant us grace, I beseech Thee, ever to teach in a teachable spirit; learning along with those we teach, and learning from them whenever Thou so pleasest. Word of God, speak to us, speak by us, what Thou wilt. Wisdom of God, instruct us, instruct by us, if and when Thou wilt. Eternal Truth, reveal Thyself to us, in whatever measure Thou wilt; that we and they may all be taught of God.

CHRISTINA ROSSETTI

July 17

FOR SCIENTISTS

O GOD, who art the goal of all knowledge and the source of all truth, who dost lead mankind towards Thyself along the paths of discovery and learning. Direct with Thy Holy Spirit the work of scientists throughout the world. Enlighten with Thy wisdom and endue with humility those engaged in the investigation of the secrets of Thy universe. Grant that they may be led through their labour to a greater knowledge of Thee, and that we may use their discoveries according to Thy will and to the benefit of our fellow men; through Jesus Christ our Lord.

THOMAS KERR

July 18

ALMIGHTY God, who hast proclaimed Thine eternal truth by the voice of prophets and evangelists: Direct and bless, we beseech Thee, those who in this generation speak where many listen and write what many read; that they may do their part in making the heart of the people wise, its mind sound, and its will righteous; to the honour of Jesus Christ our Lord.

Adapted from The Boys' Prayer Book

O God, who by Thy Spirit in our hearts dost lead men to desire Thy perfection, to seek for truths and to rejoice in beauty: illuminate and inspire, we beseech Thee, all thinkers, writers, artists and craftsmen; that, in whatsoever is true and pure and lovely, Thy name may be hallowed and Thy kingdom come on earth; through Jesus Christ our Lord.

Prayer found in St. Anselm's Chapel, Canterbury

FOR FARMERS

ALMIGHTY God, who hast blessed the earth that it should be fruitful and bring forth abundantly whatever is needful for the life of man: prosper, we pray Thee, the work of the farmer, and grant such seasonable weather that we may gather in the fruits of the earth, and ever rejoice in Thy goodness; through Jesus Christ our Lord.

DR. OSCAR HARDMAN

July 20

OFFICE HYMN FOR PRIME

Now that the daylight fills the sky,
We lift our hearts to God on high,
That He, in all we do or say,
Would keep us free from harm to-day:

Would guard our hearts and tongues from strife;
From anger's din would hide our life:
From all ill sights would turn our eyes,
Would close our ears from vanities . . .

So we when this new day is gone,
And night in turn is drawing on,
With conscience by the world unstained
Shall praise His name for victory gained.

All laud to God the Father be;
All praise, eternal Son, to Thee;
All glory, as is ever meet,
To God the holy Paraclete.

O LORD Christ, help us to maintain ourselves in simplicity and in joy, the joy of the merciful, the joy of brotherly love. Grant that, renouncing henceforth all thought of looking back, and joyful with infinite gratitude, we may never fear to precede the dawn

> to praise
> and bless
> and sing
> to Christ our Lord.

The Rule of Taizé

From the unreal lead me to the real;
from darkness lead me to light;
from death lead me to deathlessness.

Ancient Indian Prayer

BLESSED art thou, O Lord our God, the God of our fathers, who turnest the shadow of death into the morning; who hast lightened mine eyes, that I sleep not in death. O Lord, blot out as a night-mist mine iniquities. Scatter my sins as a morning cloud. Grant that I may become a child of the light, and of the day. Vouchsafe to keep me this day without sin. Uphold me when I am falling, and lift me up when I am down. Preserve this day from any evil of mine, and me from the evils of the day. Let this day add some knowledge, or good deed,

to yesterday. Oh, let me hear Thy loving-kindness in
the morning, for in Thee is my trust. Teach me to do the
thing that pleaseth Thee, for Thou art my God. Let Thy
loving Spirit lead me forth into the land of righteousness.

LANCELOT ANDREWES

July 23

> O LORD, when I awake, and day begins,
>   waken me to Thy Presence;
>   waken me to Thine indwelling;
>   waken me to inward sight of Thee,
>   and speech with Thee,
>   and strength from Thee;
>   that all my earthly walk may waken into song
>   and my spirit leap up to Thee all day, all
>   ways.
>
> O my God
>   all times are Thy times,
>   and every day Thy day,
> made lovely only with Thy light.
> Bring us, O Lord, to that blessèd eternal day
>   which Thy Son our Saviour hath won for us,
>   and to the perfect light.

ERIC MILNER-WHITE
My God my Glory

LET our prayer, O Lord, come before Thee in the morning. Thou didst take upon Thee our feeble and suffering nature; grant us to pass this day in gladness and peace, without stumbling and without stain; that reaching the eventide free from evil, we may praise Thee, the eternal King: through Thy mercy, O our God, Who art blessed, and dost live, and govern all things, world without end.

ST. ANSELM

THANKS to Thee, O God, that I have risen today,
    To the rising of this life itself;
May it be to Thine own glory, O God of every gift,
    And to the glory of my soul likewise.

O great God, aid Thou my soul
    With the aiding of Thine own mercy;
Even as I clothe my body with wool,
    Cover Thou my soul with the shadow of Thy wing.

Help me to avoid every sin,
    And the source of every sin to forsake;
And as the mist scatters on the crest of the hills,
    May each ill haze clear from my soul, O God.

The Sun Dances
Prayers from the Gaelic

July 26

LORD, give us to go blithely on our business all this day, bring us to our resting beds weary and content and undishonoured, and grant us in the end the gift of sleep.

ROBERT LOUIS STEVENSON

O God, who hast folded back the mantle of the night, to clothe us in the golden glory of the day, chase from our hearts all gloomy thoughts, and make us glad with the brightness of hope, that we may effectively aspire to unwon virtues; through Jesus Christ our Lord.

Ancient Collect

July 27

AWAKE, my Soul, and with the sun
Thy daily stage of duty run;
Shake off dull sloth, and joyful rise
To pay thy morning sacrifice.

Glory to Thee, who safe hast kept
And hast refresh'd me whilst I slept;
Grant, Lord, when I from death shall wake,
I may of endless light partake.

Lord, I my vows to Thee renew;
Scatter my sins as morning dew;
Guard my first springs of thought and will,
And with Thyself my spirit fill.

Direct, control, suggest, this day,
All I design, or do, or say;
That all my powers, with all their might,
In Thy sole glory may unite.

Praise God from Whom all blessings flow,
Praise Him, all creatures here below,
Praise Him above, ye heavenly host;
Praise Father, Son, and Holy Ghost.

BISHOP THOMAS KEN

July 28

O MAKE Thy way plain before my face. Support me this
day under all the difficulties I shall meet with. I offer
myself to Thee, O God, this day to do in me, and with
me, as to Thee seems most meet.

THOMAS WILSON

We commend unto Thee, O Lord,
    our souls and our bodies,
    our minds and our thoughts,
    our prayers and our hopes,
    our health and our work,
    our life and our death;
our parents and brothers and sisters,
    our benefactors and friends,
    our neighbours, our countrymen,
        and all Christian folk
            this day and always.

LANCELOT ANDREWES
The Private Prayers of Lancelot Andrewes

July 29

THOU, who art the true Sun of the world, evermore rising, and never going down; who, by Thy most wholesome appearing and sight dost nourish, and make joyful all things, as well that are in heaven, as also that are on earth: we beseech Thee mercifully and favourably to shine into our hearts, that the night and darkness of sin, and the mists of error on every side, being driven away, Thou brightly shining within our hearts, we may all our life long go without any stumbling or offence, and may walk as in the daytime, being pure and clean from the works of darkness, and abounding in all good works which Thou hast prepared for us to walk in.

ERASMUS

July 30

O BLESSED Jesus, who didst use Thine own most precious life for the redemption of Thy human brethren, giving no thought to ease or pleasure or worldly enrichment, but filling up all Thine hours and days with deeds of self-denying love, give me grace to-day to follow the road Thou didst first tread; and to Thy name be all the glory and the praise, even unto the end.

JOHN BAILLIE
A Diary of Private Prayer

O ETERNAL Son of God, who camest from the Father, the Fountain of light, to enlighten the darkness of the world: Shine Thou upon us this day, that in whatsoever we shall do or suffer we may be acceptable to Thy Divine Majesty; for Thy Name's sake.

JEREMY TAYLOR

O God, great and wonderful,
who hast given us a pledge of Thy promised kingdom
through the good things already bestowed upon us:
Help us to shun all evil throughout this day,
that, at its end, we may stand without reproach
before Thy holy glory
and praise Thee,
the God of our life, the lover of men;
through Jesus Christ our Lord.

Adapted from *Greek Vespers*

~~~~~~~~~~~~~~~

AUGUST
~~~~~~~~~~~~~~~

PRAYERS OF KINGS AND QUEENS

THE TRANSFIGURATION

PRAYERS IN OLD AGE

FOR SPECIAL GRACES

O THOU almighty Will
Faint are Thy children, till
    Thou come with power:
Strength of our good intents,
In our frail home, Defence,
Calm of Faith's confidence,
    Come, in this hour!

O Thou most tender Love!
Deep in our spirits move:
    Tarry, dear Guest!
Quench Thou our passion's fire,
Raise Thou each low desire,
Deeds of brave love inspire,
    Quickener and Rest!

O Light serene and still!
Come, and our spirit fill,
    Bring in the day:
Guide of our feeble sight,
Star of our darkest night,
Shine on the path of right,
    Show us the way!

KING ROBERT OF FRANCE
A.D. *c.* 1000

KING SOLOMON

O GOD of our Fathers,
　　Lord who keepest Thy mercy,
　　who madest all things by Thy word;
and by Thy wisdom formedst man,
　　that he should have dominion over all things that were
　　　　made by Thee,
　　and rule the world in holiness and righteousness,
　　and execute judgement in uprightness of soul:
Give me wisdom,
　　her that sitteth by Thee on Thy throne;
Send her forth out of the holy heavens,
and from the throne of Thy glory bid her come;
　　that being present with me she may toil with me,
　　that I may learn what is well-pleasing before Thee,
　　that in my doings she may guide me in ways of
　　　　soberness
　　and guard me in her glory;
　　henceforth and always.

The Book of Wisdom, Chapter 9

August 2

O LORD God Almighty, I charge Thee of Thy great mercy and by the token of Thy holy rood that Thou guide me to Thy will and to my soul's need better than I can myself, that above all things I may inwardly love Thee with a clear mind and clean body; for Thou art my Maker, my help and my hope.

> KING ALFRED'S *Prayer at the end of his translation of Bœthius*

If thou hast a woe tell it not to the weakling, Tell it to thy saddle-bow and ride singing forth.

> *Proverbs of Alfred*

August 3

ATTRIBUTED TO KING EDWARD VI

O GRACIOUS God and most merciful Father, who hast vouchsafed us the rich and precious jewel of Thy holy word: Assist us with Thy Spirit that it may be written in our hearts to our everlasting comfort, to reform us, to renew us according to Thine own image, to build us up and edify us into the perfect building of Thy Christ, sanctifying and increasing in us all heavenly virtues. Grant this, O heavenly Father, for the same Jesus Christ's sake.

> From the Preface to the *Geneva Bible*

HOUSEHOLD OF KING HENRY VIII

O Almighty God, who hast prepared everlasting life to all those that be Thy faithful servants: Grant unto us sure hope of the life everlasting, that we, being in this world, may have some foretaste thereof in our hearts: not by our deserving, but by the merits of our Saviour and Lord Jesus Christ.

TWO PRAYERS WHICH KING HENRY VI MADE

O Lord Jesus Christ, who didst create me, redeem me, and foreordain me unto that which I now am: Thou knowest what Thou wilt do with me: deal with me according to Thy will and Thy mercy.

O Lord Jesus Christ, who alone art wisdom: Thou knowest what things are profitable for me poor sinner: be it done unto me according to Thy mercy, as it pleases Thee and seems good to the eyes of Thy Majesty.

August 6: The Transfiguration

O GOD, who on the mount didst reveal to chosen witnesses Thine only-begotten Son wonderfully transfigured, in raiment white and glistering: Mercifully grant that we, being delivered from the disquietude of this world, may be permitted to behold the King in his beauty; who with Thee, O Father, and Thee, O Holy Ghost, liveth and reigneth, one God, world without end.

WILLIAM REED-HUNTINGDON
Book of Common Prayer
Protestant Episcopal Church in the U.S.A.

Our Lord and King, what awe fell upon your disciples when they beheld you in your glory upon the Mount. Their Master had lived with them humbly as friend and brother, but when their eyes were opened and the King of Kings shone upon them in the light of heaven they were sore afraid. We too, Lord, know you as friend and comforter and shepherd of the sheep; let us not forget the glory and power of our God and King. Teach us the same holy fear as overwhelmed your disciples. And teach us too, O Lord, the honour due to our fellow men, made in the image of our God. Let us never forget that if we could see them as they truly are, transfigured by your love for them, we should be smitten to the heart. Help us to see your image in each other, O Lord, and to worship and adore.

LADY JANE GREY, QUEEN FOR A FEW DAYS

MERCIFUL God, be Thou now unto us a strong tower of defence. Give us grace to await Thy leisure, and patiently to bear what Thou doest unto us, nothing doubting Thy goodness towards us. Therefore do with us in all things as Thou wilt: Only arm us, we beseech Thee, with Thy armour, that we may stand fast; above all things taking to us the shield of faith, praying always that we may refer ourselves wholly to Thy will, being assuredly persuaded that all Thou doest cannot but be well. And unto Thee be all honour and glory.

Written in Prison

August 8

THE DYING PRAYER OF ST. MARGARET, QUEEN OF SCOTS

LORD Jesus Christ
   who according to the will of the Father,
    through the co-operation of the Holy Ghost,
hast by Thy death given life to the world:
     Deliver me.

MARY QUEEN OF SCOTS, IN PRISON

O Lord my God, I hope in Thee;
My dear Lord Jesus, set me free;
   In chains, in pains,
     I long for Thee.
    On bended knee
  I adore Thee, implore Thee
     To set me free.

KING CHARLES I

ALL-SEEING Light and Eternal Life of all things, look upon my misery with Thine eye of mercy, and let Thine infinite power vouchsafe to limit out some portion of deliverance unto me, as unto Thee shall seem most convenient. But yet, O my God, I yield unto Thy will, and joyfully embrace what sorrow Thou wilt have me suffer. Only this much let me crave of Thee (let my craving, O Lord, be accepted of Thee, since even that proceeds from Thee)—let me crave even by the noblest title, which in my greatest affliction I may give myself, that I am Thy creature, and by Thy goodness (which is Thyself), that Thou wilt suffer some beam of Thy Majesty so to shine into my mind, that it may still depend confidently on Thee.

Written by SIR PHILIP SIDNEY but
used by Charles I

O Lord, make Thy way plain before me. Let Thy glory be my end. Thy Word my rule, and then, Thy will be done.

KING CHARLES I

PRAYER OF MADAME ELIZABETH OF FRANCE

I DO not know, O God, what may happen to me to-day, I only know that nothing will happen to me but what has been foreseen by you from all eternity, and that is sufficient, O my God, to keep me in peace. I adore your eternal designs. I submit to them with all my heart. I desire them all and accept them all. I make a sacrifice of everything. I unite this sacrifice to that of your dear Son, my Saviour, begging you by His infinite merits, for the patience in troubles, and the perfect submission which is due to you in all that you will and design for me.

Written when she was in prison,
awaiting the guillotine

August 11

O LORD our God let us hope in the protecting shadow of Thy wings. Guard us and bear us up. Bear us up Thou wilt, as tiny infants and on to our grey hairs: for when Thou art our strength, it is strength indeed, but when our strength is our own it is only weakness. With Thee our good ever lives, and when we are averted from Thee we are perverted. Let us now return to Thee, O Lord, that we may not be overturned, for with Thee lives without any defect our good which is Thyself. We have no fear that there should be no place of return, merely because by our own act we fell from it: our absence does not cause our house to fall, which is Thy Eternity.

ST. AUGUSTINE
Confessions

August 12

KEEP me, O Lord, while I tarry on this earth, in a daily serious seeking after Thee, and in a believing affectionate walking with Thee; that, when Thou comest, I may be found not hiding my talent, nor serving my flesh, nor yet asleep with my lamp unfurnished; but waiting and longing for my Lord, my glorious God, for ever and ever.

RICHARD BAXTER

O Thou Who hast prepared a place for my soul,
    Prepare my soul for that place:
        Prepare it with holiness,
            Prepare it with desire;
And even while it sojourneth upon earth
    Let it dwell in heaven with Thee
Beholding the beauty of Thy countenance,
    And the glory of Thy Saints,
        Now and forever.

BISHOP HALL OF NORWICH

August 13

Give ear unto our words, O Lord,
Consider our meditation.
Let the words of our mouth
And the meditation of our heart
Be acceptable before Thee,
O Lord, our Rock and our Redeemer.

Cast us not away from Thy presence,
And take not Thy holy spirit from us.
O cast us not off in the time of old age,
Forsake us not when our strength faileth.
Forsake us not, O Lord our God,
Be not far from us . . .
For in Thee, O Lord, do we hope.
Thou wilt answer, O Lord our God.

Jewish Prayer
Service of the Orthodox Synagogue
for the Day of Atonement

177

August 14

THE day is gone, and I give Thee thanks, O Lord. Evening is at hand, furnish it with brightness. As day has its evening so also has life; the even of life is age, age has overtaken me, furnish it with brightness. Cast me not away in the time of age; forsake me not when my strength faileth me. Even to my old age be Thou He, and even to hoar hairs carry me; do Thou make, do Thou bear, do Thou carry and deliver me. Abide with me, Lord, for it is toward evening, and the day is far spent of this fretful life. Let Thy strength be made perfect in my weakness.

LANCELOT ANDREWES
The Private Prayers of Lancelot Andrewes

August 15

LIVING or dying, Lord, I would be Thine; keep me Thine own for ever, and draw me day by day nearer to Thyself, until I be wholly filled with Thy love, and fitted to behold Thee, face to face.

EDWARD BOUVERIE PUSEY

Grant us, O Lord, not to mind earthly things, but to love things heavenly; and even now, while we are placed among things that are passing away, to cleave to those that shall abide; through Jesus Christ our Lord.

Leonine Sacramentary

O GOD, who knowest us to be set in the midst of so many and great dangers, that by reason of the frailty of our nature we cannot always stand upright: grant to us such strength and protection as may support us in all dangers, and carry us through all temptations; through Jesus Christ our Lord.

> Prayer of an Invalid Pope
> *Book of Common Prayer*

August 17

A MOTHER SUPERIOR'S PRAYER

LORD, Thou knowest better than I know myself that I am growing older, and will some day be old.

Keep me from getting talkative, and particularly from the fatal habit of thinking that I must say something on every subject and on every occasion.

Release me from craving to straighten out everybody's affairs.

Keep my mind from the recital of endless details—give me wings to come to the point.

I ask for grace enough to listen to the tales of others' pains. Help me to endure them with patience.

But seal my lips on my own aches and pains—they are increasing, and my love of rehearsing them is becoming sweeter as the years go by.

Teach me the glorious lesson that occasionally it is possible that I may be mistaken.

Keep me reasonably sweet. I do not want to be a saint—
   some of them are so hard to live with—but a sour old
   woman is one of the crowning works of the devil.
Make me thoughtful—but not moody; helpful, but not
   bossy. With my vast store of wisdom it seems a pity
   not to use it all, but Thou knowest Lord, that I want
   a few friends at the end.

Anon.

August 18

O GOD, take us not hence in the midst of our days,
Let us complete in peace the number of our years.
Verily we know that our life is frail,
That our days are as an hand-breadth.

Therefore help us,
O God of our salvation,
To live before Thee in truth and uprightness
During the years of our pilgrimage.

And when it will please Thee to take us from the earth,
Be Thou with us;
And may our souls be bound up in the bond of life
With the souls of our parents and of the righteous
Who stand before Thee in heaven.

Jewish Prayer
Service of the Orthodox Synagogue
for the Festival of Passover

August 19

O Day-spring, Brightness of Light Everlasting, and Sun of Righteousness: Come and enlighten him that sitteth in darkness and the shadow of death.

Advent Antiphon

Lord, support us all the day long of this troublous life, until the shadows lengthen and the evening comes, and the busy world is hushed and the fever of life is over and our work is done. Then in Thy mercy give us safe lodging and a holy rest and peace at the last. Amen. Lord Jesus. Amen

Anon.
Favourite prayer of Cardinal Newman

August 20

O Lord Jesus Christ, who didst hearken unto the prayer of Thy disciples and abide with them, when it was towards evening and the day was far spent: abide we pray Thee with Thine aged servants in the evening of life. Make Thyself known unto them; and whensoever they shall pass through the valley of the shadow of death, be with them unto the end.

New Every Morning

Pardon the folly of this short prayer; even for Jesus Christ's sake. And give us a good night, if it be Thy pleasure.

OLIVER CROMWELL
on his death-bed

For special graces

FAITH

O LORD, increase my faith; strengthen and confirm me in the true faith; endue me with wisdom, charity and patience in all my adversity. Sweet Jesus, say Amen.

Anon.

HOPE

O God our Maker, give songs in the night
   through the long watches of hope,
     Till the shadows flee away.
Though the watch be long,
   our hope will not sleep or be sad:
     O Lord, let there be light!

ERIC MILNER-WHITE
My God my Glory

LOVE

O God, who by love alone art great and glorious, that art present and livest with us by love alone: Grant us likewise by love to attain another self, by love to live in others, and by love to come to our glory, to see and accompany Thy love throughout all eternity.

THOMAS TRAHERNE

LOVE

O THOU, who hast so loved my soul, make me a lover of souls. Fill me with an unwearied, unclaimative love, of keen perception and strong fibre, that shall help others to do their best. Help me to be an advocate of the absent, and cast out from me the dumb spirits of nervousness or self-absorption, which hinders me from showing the love I feel. Heal my heart of all uncontrolled affection, that being inwardly cured and thoroughly cleansed, I may be made fit to love, steady to persevere. Let no sickness or cross accident, no employment or weariness, make me ungracious to those about me, but in all things make me like unto Thy Holy Jesus.

Anon.

Lord, perfect for me what is lacking of thy gifts; of faith, help Thou mine unbelief; of hope, establish my trembling hope; of love, kindle its smoking flax.

LANCELOT ANDREWES
The Private Prayers of Lancelot Andrewes

TRUTH

O GOD, whose revelation never faileth and who showest a new aspect of Thy eternal truth to each generation; Grant unto us to see the truth as Thou dost set it before us in this our day and to strive for its realization among our fellows; through Jesus Christ our Lord.

Anon.

August 24

TRUTHFULNESS

O GOD in whose holy kingdom there is nothing that
worketh evil or maketh a lie. Help us, we pray Thee, to
guard our words, to keep our promises and to speak the
truth; through Jesus Christ our Lord.

Anon.

O God, the Father of all mankind, we beseech Thee to
inspire us with such love, truth and equity, that in all
our dealings one with another we may show forth our
brotherhood in Thee; for the sake of Jesus Christ our
Lord.

Book of Common Prayer, 1928

August 25

GRACE

O MOST merciful Lord, grant to me Thy grace, that it
may be with me, and labour with me, and persevere with
me even to the end. Grant that I may always desire and
will that which is to Thee most acceptable, and most
dear. Let Thy will be mine, and my will ever follow
Thine, and agree perfectly with it. Grant to me above
all things that can be desired, to rest in Thee, and in
Thee to have my heart at peace.

THOMAS À KEMPIS

HUMILITY

O Lord Jesus Christ, in all the fullness of Thy power most gentle, in Thine exceeding grace most humble: bestow Thy mind and spirit upon us, who have nothing whereof to boast; that, clothed in true humility, we may be exalted to true greatness. Grant this, O Lord, who livest and reignest with the Father and the Spirit, one God for evermore.

CANON G. W. BRIGGS

PEACE

O God, who art peace everlasting, whose chosen reward is the gift of peace, and who hast taught us that the peacemakers are Thy children; Pour Thy peace into our souls, that everything discordant may utterly vanish, and all that makes for peace be sweet to us forever.

Mozarabic Liturgy

QUIETNESS

GRANT unto us, Almighty God, that quiet mind and patient waiting to which Thy comforting Spirit comes, that we may do Thy will and have our hearts prepared for that peace of Thine which passeth understanding; which, if we have, the storms of life will hurt us but little, and the cares of life vex us not at all, in face of which death will lose its sting and the grave its victory, and we in calm joy walk all the days of our appointed time until our great change shall come.

Anon.

Lord, by Thy divine silence, by Thy wondrous patience, by Thine adorable humility, keep me quiet and still, and possess me with Thy peace.

FATHER ANDREW

August 28

JOY

GRANT me, O Lord, the royalty of inward happiness and the serenity which comes from living close to Thee. Daily renew in me the sense of Joy, and let the Eternal Spirit of the Father dwell in my soul and body, filling every corner of my heart with light and grace, so that bearing about with me the infection of a good courage, I may be a diffuser of life, and may meet all ills and cross accidents with gallant and high-hearted happiness, giving Thee thanks always for all things.

Anon.

COURAGE

O THOU, the Captain of my salvation, strengthen me inwardly and outwardly that I may be vigorous with spiritual purpose and disposed to every virtuous and gallant undertaking. Grant that I may do valiantly in despite of slothfulness or timidity, and that neither my fear of ridicule nor my love of popularity may make me seem to like what is not right. Be Thou pleased also to fortify my spirit so that I may meet life hopefully and be able to endure everything which Thou mayest be pleased to send me.

Anon.

PERSEVERANCE

O GOD, who hast willed that the gate of mercy should stand ever open to the faithful: Mercifully bestow on us the grace of perseverance that we may never turn aside from Him who is the Way, the Truth, and the Life, our Lord and Saviour, Jesus Christ.

Gelasian Sacramentary
adapted

O God whose glorious power is ever present to strengthen our weakness, help us to lean in faith upon the might of that power whenever the sorrow and toils of life threaten to overwhelm us. Grant us patience in the small trials of everyday, and endurance in the storms of pain and grief. And grant to us, O Lord our God, that both the patience and the long-suffering may be irradiated by the joy of Christ our Lord, who is the treasure of our desiring. And so make us worthy at last, in the fellowship of His sufferings, to come to the kingdom of His saints in light.

August 31

PURITY

O Spirit, Purifier from all sin, purify the inward eyes of our nature, that we may see the light of truth, and by this light may see the Supreme Father, whom none but the pure in heart can behold. Come, O blessed Spirit of Truth, for Jesus' sake.

Anon.

O forgiving Father, who never wearieth of our repentance: Grant that we may constantly lay hold of Thy everlasting mercy and so obtain the grace to begin once more.

GERALD HEARD
adapted

SEPTEMBER

PRAISE AND THANKSGIVING

FOR TRAVELLERS. FOR DOCTORS, NURSES AND
MISSIONARIES. FOR THOSE WHO DO NOT KNOW
THE MERCY OF GOD

ANGELS

Shepherd and Sower, thou,
Now helm, and bridle now,
Wing for the heavenward flight
Of flocks all pure and bright,
Fisher of men, the blest,
Out of the world's unrest,
Out of Sin's troubled sea
Taking us, Lord, to Thee . . .
O way that leads to God,
O Word abiding aye,
O endless Light on high,
Mercy's fresh-springing flood,
Worker of all things good,
O glorious Life of all
That on their Maker call.
  Christ Jesus, hear . . .
Hymns meet for Thee, our King,
  For Thee, the Christ;
Our holy tribute, this,
For wisdom, life and bliss,
Singing in chorus meet,
Singing in concert sweet
  The Almighty Son.
We, heirs of peace unpriced,
We, who are born in Christ,
A people pure from stain,
Praise we our God again,
  Lord of our Peace!

CLEMENT OF ALEXANDRIA
1st century

Praise and thanksgiving

CAEDMON'S HYMN

Now we must praise the Ruler of Heaven,
The might of the Lord and His purpose of mind,
The work of the Glorious Father; for He
God Eternal, established each wonder,
He, Holy Creator, first fashioned the heavens
As a roof for the children of earth.
And then our Guardian, the Everlasting Lord,
Adorned this middle-earth for men.
Praise the Almighty King of Heaven.

CAEDMON
A.D. 657–680

September 2

Worthy of praise from every mouth,
of confession from every tongue,
of worship from every creature,
is Thy glorious Name, O Father, Son, and Holy Ghost:
who didst create the world in Thy grace
and by Thy compassion didst save the world.
To Thy majesty, O God, ten thousand times ten
thousand bow down and adore,
Singing and praising without ceasing, and saying
Holy, Holy, Holy, Lord God of hosts;
Heaven and earth are full of Thy praises;
Hosanna in the highest.

Nestorian Liturgy

September 3

THOUGH our mouths were full of song as the sea,
Our tongues of exultation as the fullness of its waves,
And our lips of praise as the plains of the firmament:

Though our eyes gave light as the sun and moon:
Though our hands were outspread as the eagles of
    heaven,
And our feet were swift as hinds,

Yet should we be unable to thank Thee,
O Lord our God and God of our fathers,
And to bless Thy Name for even one of the countless
    thousands
And tens of thousands
Of kindnesses which Thou hast done by our fathers and
    by us.

Jewish Prayer
Service of the Orthodox Synagogue
for the Festival of Tabernacles

September 4

LORD God Almighty, Father of our Saviour Jesus Christ,
we give thanks to Thee for all things and in all things,
because Thou hast sheltered us, Thou hast succoured us,
Thou hast kept us, Thou hast spared us, Thou hast
redeemed us unto Thyself, Thou hast helped us, Thou
hast brought us to this hour. Remember, O Lover of men,
the sowings and the increase of the land: may they grow
and multiply. Remember, O Lord, in blessing, the airs of

heaven and the fruits of the earth. Remember, O Lord, the waters of the rivers: bring them up after their right measure. Remember, O Lord, the fowls of heaven and the fishes of the sea; remember the safety of men and beasts. Remember, O Lord, the safety of Thy holy Church. Remember, O Lord Christ, the captivities of Thy people. And remember, our Master, all them that have bidden us to remember them in our prayers and supplications which we offer before Thee. Heal them that are sick, give rest unto them that have fallen asleep. For Thou art the life of us all, and the salvation of us all, and the hope of us all, and the healing of us all, and the resurrection of us all, and to Thee with Thy Father and the Holy Ghost the Life Giver we send up thanksgiving unto highest heaven, world without end.

Liturgy of the Coptic Jacobites

September 5

ACCEPT, O Lord God, our Father, the sacrifices of our thanksgiving; this, of praise, for Thy great mercies already afforded to us; and this, of prayer, for the continuance and enlargement of them; this, of penitence, for such only recompense as our sinful nature can endeavour; and this, of the love of our hearts, as the only gift Thou dost ask or desire; and all these, through the all-holy and atoning sacrifice of Jesus Christ Thy Son our Saviour.

JOHN DONNE
adapted

September 6

O GOD, who art life, wisdom, truth, bounty and blessedness, the eternal, the only true good, our God and our Lord, who art our hope and our heart's joy: we acknowledge with thanksgiving that Thou hast made us in Thine Image, and that we may direct our thoughts to Thee. Lord, make us to know Thee aright, that we may love, enjoy, and possess Thee more and more.

ST. ANSELM

September 7

GLORY be to Thee, O Heavenly Father, for our being and preservation, health and strength, understanding and memory, friends and benefactors, and for all our abilities of mind and body. Glory be to Thee for our competent livelihood, for the advantages of our education, for all known and unobserved deliverances, and for the guard which Thy holy Angels keep over us. Glory be to Thee, O Lord, O Blessed Saviour, for those ordinary gifts by which sincere Christians have in all ages been enabled to work for their salvation, for all the spiritual strength and support, comfort and illumination which we receive from Thee, and for all Thy preserving, restraining, and sanctifying grace.

BISHOP THOMAS KEN

O GOD of peace and charity! we beseech Thee holy
Lord, Almighty Father, eternal God, that we may
worship Thee with a pure heart. Let us dance before
Thee with a clean conscience, let us serve Thee with all
our strength. We bless Thee, Holy Trinity, we give
thanks to Thee, we praise Thee every day, we pray unto
Thee "Abba, Father". May our praise be sweet to Thee
and our prayer accepted.

Gallican Sacramentary

September 9

ABOVE all Thy gifts of grace, O mighty and merciful
God, we thank Thee for Thyself, for Thy holiness, Thy
justice, Thy mercy, Thy power and might, Thy glory,
Thy love and Thy presence with us. Thou art Thyself
our most urgent need, more necessary to us than the bread
we ask of Thee. We thank Thee, O Lord, for Thyself.

Anon.

September 10

I WILL magnify Thee, O God, my King, and I will praise Thy name for ever and ever.

Every day will I give thanks unto Thee, and praise Thy name for ever and ever.

Great is the Lord, and marvellous worthy to be praised: there is no end of His greatness . . .

The Lord is gracious, and merciful, long-suffering and of great goodness.

The Lord is loving unto every man, and His mercy is over all His works . . .

The Lord is nigh unto all them that call upon Him: yea, all such as call upon Him faithfully.

He will fulfil the desire of them that fear Him: He also will hear their cry and will help them . . .

Let all flesh give thanks unto His holy name for ever and ever.

Psalm 145

For travellers
For doctors, nurses and missionaries
For those who do not know the mercy
of God

FOR TRAVELLERS

To our brethren that have departed from us, or are about to depart, in whatever place, give a fair journey, whether by land or rivers, or lakes, or highways, or in whatever way they may be travelling; restore them all everywhere to a tranquil harbour, to a safe harbour; vouchsafe to be their fellow-voyager and fellow-traveller. Give them back to their friends, rejoicing to the rejoicing, healthful to the healthful. And preserve, O Lord, to the end, our sojourning also in this life, without harm and without storm.

Anon.

September 12

FOR TRAVELLERS

O GOD, the end of all our journeyings, grant to all travellers an abiding sense of tranquillity and rest. Protect them in all dangers, that attended by Thy holy angels they may arrive safely at the place whither they are going, and when this life is over attain their heavenly home; through Jesus Christ our Lord.

Anon.

Favourably receive, O Lord, our supplications for Thy servant —— who is absent on a far journey, and for whom we pour forth our prayer; entreating Thy Majesty, that Thou wilt send to him the angel of Thy goodness, who may deliver him safe and sound to his home.

Gallican Sacramentary

September 13

FOR TRAVELLERS ON THE ROADS

ALMIGHTY God, giver of life and health: guide, we pray thee, with thy wisdom all who are striving to save from injury and death the travellers on our roads. Grant to those who drive along the highways consideration for others, and to those who walk on them or play beside them thoughtful caution and care; so that without fear or disaster we all may come safely to our journey's end.

BISHOP DOUGLAS CRICK

FOR TRAVELLERS BY AIR

O ALMIGHTY God, who makest the clouds thy chariots, and walkest upon the wings of the wind: We beseech thee for all who travel by air to their several duties and destinations; that thy presence may ever be with them, to pilot, to speed, and to protect; through Jesus Christ our Lord.

ERIC MILNER-WHITE
Daily Prayer

September 15

O MOST loving God, who in the Person of Thy Son Jesus Christ didst manifest Thy love to man by relieving all manner of suffering and healing all manner of disease, grant Thy blessing, I pray, to all who in any corner of the world are serving in Christ's name:

All ministers of the gospel of Christ:

All social workers:

All missionary workers abroad:

All doctors and nurses who faithfully tend the sick. Accomplish through them Thy great purpose of goodwill to men, and grant them in their own hearts the joy of Christ's most real presence.

JOHN BAILLIE
A Diary of Private Prayer

September 16

ALMIGHTY God, whose blessed Son Jesus Christ went about doing good, and healing all manner of sickness and all manner of disease among the people: Continue, we beseech Thee, that his gracious work among us; cheer, heal, and sanctify the sick; to doctors and nurses grant skill, sympathy, and patience; and send down Thy blessing on all who labour to prevent suffering, and to forward Thy purposes of love; through Jesus Christ our Lord.

Book of Common Prayer, 1928

September 17

O LORD Christ, we pray for all whom you have called to carry the knowledge of your love into all the world. We pray that your redeeming power may be with them, and that into whatever darkness of fear and suffering their way of sacrifice may lead them they may bring light, and the newness of life that comes with the rising upon us of the sun of the world. We pray especially for those who are in danger, that they may have courage and peace of mind, and for those in perplexity, that your will may be made plain to them. And we pray for those who are overworked, or lonely, ill or disheartened, that they may know the comfort and strength of your presence with them, even unto the end of the world. Grant, O Lord, that we who live far from their hardships and dangers may keep them in our hearts and prayers at all times, and obedient to your Holy Spirit may do for them all that our love can devise. Lord, bless all their work for you, and bless them and all for whom they labour, and we who pray for them, and bring us all at last, by the power of your Cross, to the full knowledge of your Love.

September 18

O GOD, who hast made of one blood all nations of men for to dwell on the face of the earth, and didst send Thy blessed Son Jesus Christ to preach peace to them that are afar off, and to them that are nigh: Grant that all the peoples of the world may feel after Thee and find Thee; and hasten, O God, the fulfilment of Thy promise, to pour out Thy Spirit upon all flesh; through Jesus Christ our Lord.

BISHOP COTTON OF CALCUTTA

September 19

O SAVIOUR of the world, teach us how to pray for those who are lost in desolations of darkness without the knowledge of the mercy that is yourself. We remember the innocent victims of war and all the agony they suffer, those who are sunk in the wretchedness of sin and can find no deliverance, those in despair, those beset by temptation, those who are greatly afraid, those who have been overwhelmed by torment of mind or body. Save us from the cowardice that would turn away from the thought of these things, from the indifference that would pass them by. Give us penitence for the evil in ourselves which has added to the darkness of the world, and if there be any small thing we can do to lighten any misery, show us what it is and help us to do it. Teach us how to pray with the compassion which is not afraid to suffer with those who suffer and, if need be, to enter into darkness with them. O Everlasting Mercy, who once in time came from the height of heaven down to the depth of our need, come again in power to forgive us and renew us and set us on fire, that through the labours and prayers of broken-hearted sinners your mercy may banish the darkness and bring new life upon the earth.

September 20

Look in compassion, O Heavenly Father, upon this troubled and divided world. Though we cannot trace Thy footsteps or understand Thy working, give us grace to trust Thee now with an understanding faith, and when Thine own time is come, reveal, O Lord, Thy new heaven and new earth, wherein dwelleth righteousness, and where the Prince of Peace ruleth, Thy Son our Saviour Jesus Christ.

DEAN VAUGHAN

Angels

Iᴛ is very meet, right, and our bounden duty, that we should at all times, and in all places, give thanks unto Thee, O Lord, Holy Father, Almighty, Everlasting God.

Therefore with Angels and Archangels, and with all the company of heaven, we laud and magnify Thy glorious Name; evermore praising Thee, and saying,

Holy, Holy, Holy, Lord God of hosts; heaven and earth are full of thy glory. Glory be to thee, O Lord most High.

Book of Common Prayer

Bʏ the prayer and supplication of the angels of peace and love, we ask,

From Thee, O Lord,

Night and day and all the days of our life, eternal peace for Thy Church and a life without sin.

From Thee, O Lord,

Remission of sins, and that which may be profitable to our life, and well-pleasing to Thy Divinity we ask,

From Thee, O Lord.

The mercy of the Lord and His loving-kindness, ever and at all times we ask,

From Thee, O Lord.

Let us commend ourselves and our souls to the Father the Son and the Holy Spirit:

To Thee, O Lord God.

Liturgy of Malabar

September 23

LORD, who hast died for us, beside whose awful mercy we confess that he who is not burned with love needeth to be purged with tears: Grant us such penitence as may be no reproach to us before Thine angels, and such love as shall carry us into their choirs; which praise Thee with the Father and the Holy Ghost, God most glorious, for ever.

ERIC MILNER-WHITE
A Cambridge Bede Book

September 24

O GOD, who by Thy Angels, didst bring the joyful tidings of the birth of Christ,
   Have mercy upon us.
Thou who by Thy angel didst strengthen Jesus in His agony,
   Have mercy upon us.
Thou who didst bid Thy Angels to watch at the tomb of Jesus,
   Have mercy upon us.
Thou who didst send Thy Angels to proclaim the Ascension of Jesus,
   Have mercy upon us.
That it may please Thee to fill us with love for those glorious spirits,
   We beseech Thee to hear us.
That it may please Thee by the ministry of thy Angels to keep us in all our ways,
   We beseech Thee to hear us.

That it may please Thee that after our death the Angels
may carry our souls into Thy rest,
>   We beseech Thee to hear us.
Praise the Lord, ye Angels of His, ye servants of His that
do His pleasure.

A Book of Litanies

September 25

O EVERLASTING God, who hast ordained and con-
stituted the services of Angels and men in a wonderful
order; Mercifully grant, that as Thy holy Angels always
do Thee service in heaven, so by Thy appointment they
may succour and defend us on earth; through Jesus
Christ our Lord.

Book of Common Prayer

September 26

LET thy mercy be upon us, O Lord, cleanse our defilement, sanctify our lips, and let the voices of our foolish-
ness mingle with the praises of seraphim and archangels
glorifying Thy love: for herein Thou hast associated
mortal man with spirits. With these heavenly hosts
then, we, Thy poor weak and useless servants, praise
Thee, my Lord, because of Thy great mercy towards us,
for which we cannot render Thee due thanks.

Liturgy of Malabar

September 27

PRAYER TO THE GOOD ANGEL

O MY Lord Jesus Christ, as it hath pleased Thee to assign an angel to wait on me daily and nightly, with great attendance and diligence, so I beseech Thee, through his going betwixt us, that Thou cleanse me from vices, clothe me with virtues, grant me love and grace to come, see, and have without end Thy bliss, before Thy fair face, that liveth and reigneth after Thy glorious passion with the Father of heaven, and with the Holy Ghost, one God and Persons three, without end in bliss.

Processional of the Nuns of Chester

September 28

THE GUARDIAN ANGEL

THOU angel of God who hast charge of me
From the dear Father of mercifulness,
The shepherding kind of the fold of the saints
To make round about me this night;

Drive from me every temptation and danger,
Surround me on the sea of unrighteousness,
And in the narrows, crooks, and straits,
Keep thou my coracle, keep it always.

Be thou a bright flame before me,
Be thou a guiding star above me,
Be thou a smooth path below me,
And be a kindly shepherd behind me,
Today, tonight, and for ever.

I am tired and I a stranger,
Lead thou me to the land of angels;
For me it is time to go home
To the court of Christ, to the peace of heaven.

The Sun Dances
Prayers from the Gaelic

PRAYER OF THE GUARDIAN ANGEL

O LORD, how wonderful in depth and light,
  But most in man, how wonderful Thou art!
With what a love, with what persuasive might
  Victorious o'er the stubborn fleshly heart,
Thy tale complete of saints Thou dost provide,
To fill the thrones which angels lost through pride! . . .

O man, strange composite of heaven and earth!
  Majesty dwarfed to baseness! fragrant flower
Running to poisonous seed! and seeming worth
  Cloking corruption! weakness mastering power!
Who never art so near to crime and shame,
As when Thou hast achieved some deed of name—

How should ethereal natures comprehend
  A thing made up of spirit and of clay,
Were we not tasked to nurse it and to tend,
  Linked one to one throughout its mortal day?
More than the Seraph in his height of place,
The Angel-guardian knows and loves the ransomed race.

CARDINAL NEWMAN
The Dream of Gerontius

September 30

Jesu! by that shuddering dread which fell on Thee;
Jesu! by that cold dismay which sickened Thee;
Jesu! by that pang of heart which thrilled in Thee;
Jesu! by that mount of sins which crippled Thee;
Jesu! by that sense of guilt which stifled Thee;
Jesu! by that innocence which girded Thee;
Jesu! by that sanctity which reigned in Thee;
Jesu! by that Godhead which was one with Thee;
Jesu! spare these souls which are so dear to Thee,
Who in prison, calm and patient, wait for Thee;
Hasten, Lord, their hour, and bid them come to Thee,
To that glorious Home, where they shall ever gaze on
    Thee.

CARDINAL NEWMAN
The Dream of Gerontius

THE CHOIR OF ANGELICALS

Praise to the Holiest in the height,
    And in the depths be praise:
In all his words most wonderful;
    Most sure in all his ways!

CARDINAL NEWMAN
The Dream of Gerontius

OCTOBER

FOR ANIMALS

FOR OURSELVES WHEN WE ARE SICK OR SORRY

EVENING PRAYERS

As proud of a penny as of a pound of gold,
And as glad of a garment of russet grey
As of a silken tunic of scarlet tint.
He rejoices with the joyful, and is generous to the wicked,
Loving and believing in all that our Lord made . . .
All manner of mischiefs he mildly suffers,
Coveting no earthly good, but the joy of heaven.
Fiat voluntas tua will always find him.
He tends, at other times, to take a pilgrimage
To seek pardon of the poor, and of those in prison.
Though he brings them no bread, he bears them sweeter
    life,
Loving them as our Lord has bidden, looking how they
    are . . .
For Charity is God's champion, a cheerful child,
The merriest of mouth when he sits at meat.
The love that lies in his heart has made him light of
    speech,
Comforting and companionable, as Christ Himself bade.
I have seen him in silk, and in coarsest cloth,
Grey or gaudy, or in gilt harness,
And as gladly he gave it to good fellows needing it . . .
And in a friar's frock he was found once,
But it was far away, in Saint Francis' time . . .

WILLIAM LANGLAND
Visions from Piers Plowman

For animals

HAVE pity, O Lord God, lest they who go by the way trample on the unfledged bird, and send Thine Angel to replace it in the nest, that it may live till it can fly.

ST. AUGUSTINE

For those, O Lord, the humble beasts, that bear with us the burden and heat of the day, and offer their guileness lives for the well-being of their countries; and for the wild creatures, whom thou hast made wise, strong and beautiful; we supplicate for them Thy great tenderness of heart, for thou hast promised to save both man and beast, and great is thy loving kindness, O Master, Saviour of the world.

Eastern Church

WE beseech thee, O God, to hear our supplications on behalf of the dumb creation, who after their kind, bless, praise and magnify Thee forever. Grant that all cruelty may cease out of our land; and deepen our thankfulness to Thee for the faithful companionship of those whom we delight to call our friends; according to the loving-kindness of our Lord Jesus Christ.

Prayer of the R.S.P.C.A.

October 3

ANIMALS USED IN VIVISECTION

O GOD our Creator, who hast given to the world so many creatures of infinite beauty and variety, for the enrichment of life and the increase of joy, grant to us all a deep and humble reverence for the creatures that you have made. Give us penitence for all the ways in which we misuse them, and when their use seems unavoidable grant that we may treat them with love and compassion. Especially we pray for love in the practice of vivisection. Help us to use it as little as possible, with reverent care, and gratitude to the animals who give their lives to save ours. We remember especially the dogs who suffered that insulin might bring relief to thousands, and those animals who have been used to deliver a multitude of children from polio, and those who are being used now in the fight against cancer. We thank you for them, and if this thing must be for a time, we beseech you to shorten the time and show us a better way.

PRAYERS FOR THE DAY OF ST. FRANCIS
OF ASSISI

O GOD, who, by the merits of the blessed Francis, hast enriched Thy Church with a new offspring; grant that, in imitation of him, we may despise the things of this world, and ever find pleasure in the participation of Thy heavenly gifts.

Anon.

All ye works of the Lord, bless ye the Lord. Let us praise and exalt Him above all forever.

Give praise to God all ye His servants and you that fear Him, little and great. Let us praise and exalt him above all forever.

Let the heavens and the earth praise him, the Glorious, and every creature which is in heaven and on earth and under the earth, in the seas and all that are in them. Let us praise and exalt him above all forever.

ST. FRANCIS OF ASSISI

October 5

HEAR our humble prayer, O God, for our friends the animals, Thy creatures. We pray especially for all that are suffering in any way; for the overworked and underfed, the hunted, lost or hungry; for all in captivity or ill-treated, and for those who must be put to death.

We entreat for them Thy mercy and pity; and for those who deal with them we ask a heart of compassion, gentle hands and kindly words.

Make us all to be true friends to animals and so more worthy followers of our merciful Saviour, Jesus Christ.

Anon.
A Prayer commended by the late Bishop Kirk of Oxford

October 6

LITANY FOR THE ANIMALS

ALMIGHTY and loving Creator, for the whole animal creation which thou hast given for our enjoyment and use,

We worship Thee and thank Thee.

Purge from all cruelty the heart of mankind and give love and caring for all Thy creatures.

O Everlasting Mercy, hear us.

For all animals driven to slaughter in every country in the world. Put Thy mercy in the men who do this work; protect the animals from violence and thirst.

O Lord, hear our prayer.

Good Lord, succour and protect all animals travelling by land, sea and air, by rail and road, and be in the men who should care for them.

Hear our prayer, we beseech Thee.

For all beasts of burden, labour and toil in all the ways they go; touch their worn bodies, heal their wounds, ease their burdens and strengthen their limbs. We pray for every man, woman and child who goes with them—that Thou wilt keep them from cruelty.

O Lord, we beseech Thee to hear us.

Almighty, merciful and loving God, receive the prayer we bring and by the mystery of Thy ways, transmute it into power to redeem Thy creatures from suffering and bring them to a life of happiness and peace, that Thou mayest be glorified through all time and eternity.

A shortened form of a *Litany for the Animals*
composed by NORAH THOMPSON

PRAYER FOR MOTHS

When
—At the mid of moon,
At end of day—
My lamp is lit,
Grant me a boon,
I pray,
And do
So order it

—That the small creatures,
Terrified and blind;
The gold and silvern moths
Of lovely kind,
Do not whirl to my taper,
Nor, therein,
Die, painfully,
And bring my light
To sin.

My light
is innocent!
Grant
—That it may be
Harmless,
And helpful,
And remarked
Of Thee.

JAMES STEPHENS
Student Taper

PRAYER OF THE LARK

I AM here! O my God.
I am here, I am here!
You drew me away from earth,
and I climb to You
in a passion of shrilling,
To the dot in heaven
Where, for an instant, You crucify me.
When will You keep me forever?
Must You always let me fall
back to the furrow's dip,
a poor bird of clay?
Oh, at least
let my exultant nothingness
soar to the glory of Your mercy,
in the same hope,
until death.

CARMEN BERNOS DE GASZTOLD
Prayers from the Ark

PRAYER OF THE TORTOISE

A LITTLE patience,
O God,
I am coming.
One must take nature as she is!
It was not I who made her!
I do not mean to criticize

this house on my back—
it has its points—
but you must admit, Lord,
it is heavy to carry!
Still,
let us hope that this double enclosure,
my shell and my heart,
will never be quite shut to You.

CARMEN BERNOS DE GASZTOLD
Prayers from the Ark

October 10

PRAYER OF THE OLD HORSE

SEE, Lord,
my coat hangs in tatters,
like homespun, old, threadbare.
All that I had of zest,
all my strength,
I have given in hard work
and kept nothing back for myself.
Now
my poor head swings
to offer up all the loneliness of my heart.
Dear God,
stiff on my thickened legs
I stand here before You:
Your unprofitable servant.
Oh! of Your goodness,
give me a gentle death.

CARMEN BERNOS DE GASZTOLD
Prayers from the Ark

For ourselves when we are sick or sorry

October 11

HELP me, O Lord, so to strive and so to act, that those things which cloud my own way may not darken the path which others have to tread. Give me unselfish courage so that I am ready always to share my bread and wine, and able to hide my hunger and thirst.

LESLIE D. WEATHERHEAD
A Private House of Prayer

October 12

WRITE Thy blessed name, O Lord, upon my heart, there to remain so indelibly engraved, that no prosperity, no adversity shall ever move me from Thy love. Be Thou to me a strong Tower of defence, a Comforter in tribulation, a Deliverer in distress, a very present Help in trouble, and a Guide to heaven through the many temptations and dangers of this life.

THOMAS À KEMPIS

Lord, teach me the art of patience whilst I am well, and give me the use of it when I am sick. In that day either lighten my burden or strengthen my back. Make me, who so often in my health have discovered my weakness presuming on my own strength, to be strong in my sickness when I rely solely on Thy assistance.

THOMAS FULLER

October 13

IN confidence of Thy goodness and great mercy, O Lord, I draw near unto Thee, as a sick person to the Healer, as one hungry and thirsty to the Fountain of life, a creature to the Creator, a desolate soul to my own tender Comforter. Behold, in Thee is all whatsoever I can or ought to desire; Thou art my Salvation and my Redemption, my Help and my Strength. Rejoice therefore this day the soul of Thy servant; for unto Thee, O Lord, have I lifted up my soul.

THOMAS À KEMPIS

October 14

O GOD, who hast exalted the Crucified, the Son, by a triumphant resurrection and ascension into heaven: May His triumphs and glories so shine in the eyes of our hearts and minds, that we may more clearly comprehend His sufferings, and more courageously pass through our own; for His sake who with Thee and the Holy Ghost liveth and reigneth, one God, for ever and ever.

ERIC MILNER-WHITE
A Cambridge Bede Book

WITH floods and storms thus we be tossed,
    Awake, good Lord, to Thee we cry.
Our ship is almost sunk and lost.
Thy mercy help our misery.
    Man's strength is weak: man's wit is dull:
Man's reason blind. These things t'amend,
Thy hand, O Lord, of might is full;
Awake betime, and help us send.
    In Thee we trust, and in no wight:
Save us as chickens under the hen.
Our crookedness Thou canst make right,
Glory to Thee for aye. Amen

Anon.

October 16

ALMIGHTY and everlasting God, mercifully look upon our infirmities, and in all our dangers and necessities stretch forth Thy right hand to help and defend us; through Jesus Christ our Lord.

Book of Common Prayer

O living Christ, make us conscious now of Thy healing nearness. Touch our eyes that we may see Thee; open our ears that we may hear Thy voice; enter our hearts that we may know Thy love. Overshadow our souls and bodies with Thy presence, that we may partake of Thy strength, Thy love and Thy healing life.

HOWARD CHANDLER ROBBINS

October 17

LORD, since Thou hast taken from me all that I had of Thee, yet of Thy grace leave me the gift which every dog has by nature; that of being true to Thee in my distress, when I am deprived of all consolation. This I desire more fervently than Thy heavenly Kingdom!

MECHTHILD OF MAGDEBURG
Light of the Godhead

O Lord, Jesus Christ, who art as the Shadow of a Great Rock in a weary land, who beholdest Thy weak creatures weary of labour, weary of pleasure, weary of hope deferred, weary of self; in Thine abundant compassion, and fellow feeling with us, and unutterable tenderness, bring us, we pray Thee, unto Thy rest.

CHRISTINA ROSSETTI

October 18

MAY I taste that communion, Lord,
   Thy people have with Thee?
Thy Spirit daily talks with them,
   O let it talk with me!

Like Enoch, let me walk with God,
   And thus walk out my day,
Attended with the heavenly Guards,
   Upon the King's highway.

When wilt Thou come unto me, Lord?
   O come, my Lord most dear!
Come near, come nearer, nearer still:
   I'm well when Thou art near.

When wilt Thou come unto me, Lord?
   For, till Thou dost appear,
I count each moment for a day,
   Each minute for a year.

THOMAS SHEPHERD

October 19

AH God! behold my grief and care. Fain would I serve Thee with a glad and cheerful countenance, but I cannot do it. However much I fight and struggle against my sadness, I am too weak for this sore conflict. Help me in my weakness, O Thou mighty God.

S. SCHERETZ

I am Thine; save me. Behold, O Lord, I am Thy servant and the son of Thine handmaid; an unprofitable servant, yet a servant; a lost son, yet a son. We are all Thy people. Carest Thou not that we perish? Yea, Thou carest.

LANCELOT ANDREWES
The Private Prayers of Lancelot Andrewes

October 20

THE Lord is my light, and my salvation; whom then shall I fear? The Lord is the strength of my life; of whom then shall I be afraid? . . .

For in the time of trouble He shall hide me in His tabernacle; yea, in the secret place of His dwelling shall He hide me, and set me up upon a rock of stone . . .

I should utterly have fainted but that I believe verily to see the goodness of the Lord in the land of the living.

O tarry thou the Lord's leisure; be strong, and He shall comfort thine heart; and put thou thy trust in the Lord.

Psalm 27

October 21

THANKSGIVING FOR RECOVERY FROM ILLNESS

O GOD, great, mighty, and revered,
In the abundance of Thy lovingkindness,
    I come before Thee
To render thanks
    For all the benefits Thou hast bestowed upon me.

In my distress I called upon Thee
    And Thou didst answer me;
From my bed of pain I cried unto Thee
    And Thou didst hear the voice of my supplication.
Thou hast chastened me sore, O Lord,
    But Thou didst not give me over unto death.

In Thy love and pity
>Thou broughtest up my soul from the grave.
For Thine anger is but for a moment;
>Thy favour is for a lifetime;
Weeping may tarry for the night,
>But joy cometh in the morning.

The living,
The living,
He shall praise Thee,
>As I do this day,
And my soul that Thou didst redeem
>Shall tell Thy wonders unto the children of men.
Blessed art Thou,
>The faithful physician unto all flesh.

Jewish Prayer
Authorized Daily Prayer Book

October 22

WATCH Thou, dear Lord, with those who wake and watch or weep tonight, and give thine angels charge over those who sleep. Tend Thy sick ones, O Lord Christ; rest Thy weary ones; bless Thy dying ones; soothe Thy suffering ones; shield Thy joyous ones; and all for Thy Love's sake.

ST. AUGUSTINE

Be present, O merciful God, and protect us through the silent hours of this night, so that we who are fatigued by the changes and chances of this fleeting world, may repose upon Thy eternal changelessness.

Leonine Sacramentary

October 23

SHEPHERD who dost not sleep, keep watch and ward over Thy flock of souls.
     Amen.
And that it be not disturbed by terror of the night, sanctify it by the unseen touch of Thy hand.
     Amen.
Make the frail stalwart, lift up the contrite, make the weak strong. Raise up by piety, build up by charity, purify by chastity, illuminate by wisdom, save by pity.
     Amen.

Let watchful faith win the reward of constancy in Thy love, temperance of habit, providence in mercy, discipline of conduct.

Amen.

In Thy merciful compassion shut not out from the splendour of Thy promise, but lead to pardon, him whom Thou hast made Thine own by grace.

Amen.

Gothic Missal

October 24

OFFICE HYMN FOR COMPLINE

BEFORE the ending of the day,
Creator of the world, we pray
That with Thy wonted favour Thou
Wouldst be our Guard and Keeper now.

From all ill dreams defend our eyes,
From nightly fears and fantasies;
Tread under foot our ghostly foe,
That no pollution we may know.

O Father, that we ask be done,
Through Jesus Christ, Thine only Son;
Who, with the Holy Ghost and Thee,
Doth live and reign eternally.

Anon.

October 25

INTO Thy hands, most blessed Jesus, I commend my soul and body. So bless and sanctify my sleep unto me, that it may be temperate, holy, and safe, a refreshment to my wearied body, to enable it to serve my soul, that both may serve Thee with a never-failing duty, and that whether I sleep or wake, I may be Thy servant and Thy child.

Anon.

October 26

BLESSED art Thou, O Lord our God, King of the
  universe,
Who makest the bands of sleep to fall upon mine eyes
And slumber upon mine eyelids.

May it be Thy will, O Lord my God and God of my
  fathers,
To suffer me to lie down in peace
And to let me rise up again in peace.

Let not my thoughts trouble me,
Nor evil dreams, nor evil fancies,
But let my rest be perfect before Thee.

O lighten my eyes, lest I sleep the sleep of death,
For it is Thou who givest light to the apple of the eye.
Blessed art Thou, O Lord,
Who givest light to the whole world in Thy glory.

Jewish Prayer
Authorized Daily Prayer Book

GLORY to Thee, my God, this night
For all the blessings of the light;
Keep me, O keep me, King of kings,
Beneath Thine own almighty wings.

Forgive me, Lord, for Thy dear Son,
The ill that I this day have done,
That with the world, myself, and Thee,
I, ere I sleep, at peace may be.

Teach me to live, that I may dread
The grave as little as my bed;
Teach me to die, that so I may
Rise glorious at the awful day.

Praise God, from whom all blessings flow,
Praise him, all creatures here below,
Praise him above, ye heavenly host,
Praise Father, Son, and Holy Ghost.

BISHOP THOMAS KEN

October 28

O LORD God, who art light eternal, in the brightness of whose countenance is day that knows no night, and in Thy protecting arms all quietness and tranquillity: Whilst the darkness covers the face of the earth, receive our body and soul unto Thy care and keeping; that whether we sleep or wake, we may rest in Thee, in Thy light beholding light; through Jesus Christ our Lord.

JEREMY TAYLOR

October 29

O GOD, hearken to my prayer,
Let my earnest petition come to Thee,
For I know that Thou art hearing me
As surely as though I saw Thee with mine eyes.

Let no fancy come to my mind,
Let no ruffle come to my spirit,
That is hurtful to my poor body this night,
Nor ill for my soul at the hour of my death;

But mayest Thou Thyself, O God of life,
Be at my breast, be at my back,
Thou to me as a star, Thou to me as a guide,
From my life's beginning to my life's closing.

The Sun Dances
Prayers from the Gaelic

O LORD Jesus Christ, our Watchman and Keeper, take us to Thy care: grant that, our bodies sleeping, our minds may watch in Thee, and be made merry by some sight of that celestial and heavenly life wherein Thou art the King and Prince, together with the Father and the Holy Spirit, where Thy angels and holy souls be most happy citizens. Oh purify our souls, keep clean our bodies, that in both we may please Thee, sleeping and waking, for ever.

A Booke of Christian Prayers

Now that night is creeping
O'er our travail'd senses,
To Thy care unsleeping
We commit our sleep.
Nature for a season
Conquers our defences,
But th'eternal Reason
Watch and ward will keep.

All the soul we render
Back to Thee completely,
Trusting Thou wilt tend her
Through the deathlike hours,
And all night remake her
To Thy likeness sweetly,
Then with dawn awake her
And give back her powers.

Slumber's less uncertain
Brother soon will bind us
—Darker falls the curtain,
Stifling-close 'tis drawn:
But amidst the prison
Still Thy voice can find us,
And, as Thou hast risen,
Raise us in Thy dawn.

C. S. LEWIS
Poems

NOVEMBER

ALL SAINTS

ALL SOULS. THOSE WHO MOURN. THE HOPE OF HEAVEN
PRAYERS OF THE SAINTS

A SAINT

BEFORE St. Anno
Six were sainted
Of our holy bishops.
Like the seven stars
They shall shine from heaven.
Purer and brighter
Is the light of Anno
Than a hyacinth set in a gold ring!

This darling man
We will have for a pattern;
And those that would grow
In virtue and trustiness
Shall dress by him as at a mirror.

As the sun in the air
Between earth and heaven
Glitters to both—
So went Bishop Anno
Between God and man.

Such was his virtue in the palace
That the emperor obeyed him;
He behaved with honour to both sides
And was counted among the first barons.

In his gestures at worship
He was awful as an angel.
Many a man knew his goodness.
Hear what were his manners—
His words were frank and open;
He spoke truth fearing no man;
Like a lamb he sat among princes,
Like a lamb he walked among the people;
To the unruly he was sharp;
To the gentle he was mild;
Widows and orphans praised him always.

Preaching and praying
No one could do better.
Happy was Cologne
To be worthy of such a bishop!

Anon.
10th century

All Saints

COME in peace, ye Prophets of the Spirit, who have prophesied concerning our Redeemer. Come in peace, ye chosen Apostles, who have preached the good news of the Only-begotten. Come in peace, ye Martyrs, friends of the heavenly Bridegroom. Come in peace, all ye Saints, friends of the Son. Offer to Him your prayers for us, that He for whose sake ye travailed may be merciful to us at your intercession, O ye holy ones.

Maronite Liturgy

O ALMIGHTY God, who hast knit together Thine elect in one communion and fellowship, in the mystical body of Thy Son Christ our Lord: Grant us grace so to follow Thy blessed saints in all virtuous and godly living, that we may come to those unspeakable joys, which Thou hast prepared for them that unfeignedly love Thee, through Jesus Christ our Lord.

Book of Common Prayer

November 3

GLORY be to the Eternal Mercy which sent Thee unto us, O Christ, the light of the world and the life of all; forever Thy servants take refuge in faith, hiding themselves under the wings of the Cross. Keep by Thy compassion the company of Thy worshippers, and account us worthy, O Lord, with Thy Saints to sing to Thee; may we confess Thee and praise Thee without ceasing in Thy crowned Church which is full of helps and blessings. O Holy, Glorious, Mighty, and Immortal, who dwellest in the saints; turn, O Lord, and have mercy upon us, as Thou art wont at all times; for Thou art Lord and Creator of all, Father, Son, and Holy Ghost, forever.

Liturgy of the Nestorians

November 4

WE thank Thee, O Lord, for all who have chosen poverty or solitude for Thy sake, for men of prayer, for saints in common life who have borne suffering for noble ends, and for those who have endured pain with patience and purity of life, in the strength of Him who for the joy that was set before Him endured the Cross, ever Jesus Christ our Lord.

Anon.

All souls
Those who mourn
The hope of Heaven

November 5

O God, who hast brought us near to an innumerable
company of angels, and to the spirits of just men made
perfect: Grant us during our earthly pilgrimage to abide
in their fellowship, and in our heavenly country to
become partakers of their joy; through Jesus Christ our
Lord.

WILLIAM BRIGHT

O Father of all, we pray to Thee for those whom we
love, but see no longer. Grant them Thy peace; let
light perpetual shine upon them; and in Thy loving
wisdom and almighty power work in them the good
purpose of Thy perfect will; through Jesus Christ our
Lord.

Book of Common Prayer, 1928

November 6

HAVE mercy, O Lord, on those who have slept and rested in the faith of Christ. Feed them in green pastures, by the waters of comfort, in the Paradise of joy; the place whence all sorrow and sighing and weeping have fled away in the light of Thy saints. Grant them the good things which eye hath not seen, nor ear heard, neither have they entered into the heart of man, which Thou, God, hast prepared for them that love Thy holy Name. Remit their sins, for there is no one clean and without blemish; give them rest and make them worthy of the Kingdom of Heaven.

Liturgy of St. Mark

November 7

O LORD Jesus, who knowest them that are Thine;
    When Thou rewardest Thy servants the prophets, remember we beseech Thee, for good those who have taught us, counselled us, guided us,
    and in that day show them mercy:
    When Thou rewardest the saints, remember, we beseech Thee, for good those who have surrounded us with holy influences, borne with us, forgiven us, sacrificed themselves for us, loved us,
    and in that day show them mercy;
Nor forget any, nor forget us,
    but in that day show us mercy,
        O Lord, Thou lover of souls.

CHRISTINA ROSSETTI

GIVE rest, O Christ, to Thy servant with Thy Saints: where sorrow and pain are no more; neither sighing, but life everlasting.

Thou only art immortal, the Creator and Maker of man: and we are mortal, formed of the earth, and unto earth shall we return: for so Thou didst ordain, when Thou createdst me, saying, Dust thou art, and unto dust shalt thou return. All we go down to the dust; and, weeping o'er the grave, we make our song: alleluya, alleluya, alleluya.

Give rest, O Christ, to Thy servant with Thy Saints, where sorrow and pain are no more; neither sighing, but life everlasting.

Russian Contakion of the Departed

A MEMORIAL PRAYER

O LORD our God, through whose love we have our being and in whose presence is eternal life, in this solemn hour we remember before Thee, all those whose lives in this world claim our love and affection, admiration, respect and gratitude, and whom Thou hast now taken to eternity.

We recall the great of mankind who in signal measure have pointed the way as leaders of men and nations. We think of the heroes and martyrs, especially of the House of Israel but also of all the families of the earth, the witnesses to thy holy spirit in the world . . . May their names shine as the stars in heaven forever and forever.

Oh our merciful Father, we recall before Thee, each one of us, those who are nearest and dearest to us . . . In the holy quiet of the Sanctuary, the names and the qualities of them all are counted over with tender longing. Each capacity, each merit and each grace shines before us now as a crown to a treasured name and as an incentive to rich and noble living . . .

May the voice of reason speak to our troubled spirits of the essential place of death in the scheme of life . . . We could know no life of meaning and worth except through the pilgrimage of struggle which is the earthly lot of us all . . . May the light of faith pierce the shadows that enfold us, and still the storm of our rebellion. May we be a little more content when our questions are not answered. May we be wise enough to sense the over-mastering mystery which no human mind can penetrate. In God's holy presence we would subdue arrogance, and resign ourselves to a higher will. In the dwelling place of everlasting love, may we seek our rest—and our comfort in the faith that all souls, theirs and ours, are bound up in the bundle of life.

Jewish Prayer
West London Synagogue Prayer Book

November 10

O ALMIGHTY God, the God of the spirits of all flesh: Multiply, we beseech Thee, to those who rest in Jesus, the manifold blessings of Thy love, that the good work which Thou didst begin in them may be perfected unto the day of Jesus Christ. And of Thy mercy, O heavenly

Father, vouchsafe that we who now serve Thee here on earth may, at the last, together with them, be found meet to be partakers of the inheritance of the saints in light; for the sake of the same Thy Son Jesus Christ our Lord and Saviour.

Book of Common Prayer
Episcopal Church of Scotland

November 11

FOR Thy happy servants, our fathers and brethren, who have departed this life with the seal of faith, we praise and magnify Thy holy name; most humbly desiring that we may still continue in their holy communion, and enjoy the comfort thereof, following, with a glad will and mind, their holy examples of godly living, and steadfastness in Thy faith.

Private Devotions
16th century

November 12

O THOU Good Omnipotent, who so carest for every one of us, as if Thou caredst for him alone; and so for all, as if all were but one! Blessed is the man who loveth Thee, and his friend in Thee, and his enemy for Thee. For he only loses none dear to Him, to whom all are dear in Him who cannot be lost. To Thee will I intrust whatsoever I have received from Thee, so shall I lose nothing. Thou madest me for Thyself, and my heart is restless until it repose in Thee.

ST. AUGUSTINE

243

November 13

O GOD, the God of the spirits of all flesh in whose care all souls live, in whatsoever world or condition they may be; I beseech Thee for him whose name, and dwelling place, and every need Thou knowest. Lord, grant to him light and rest, peace and refreshment, joy and consolation in the nearness of the Saviour, in the companionship of saints, in the ample folds of Thy great love. Grant that he may go from strength to strength until at last he can enjoy the unveiled vision of Thy glory.

If it may be, tell him, gracious Lord, how much I love him and miss him and long to see him again, and if there be ways in which he may come, grant him to me as a guide and guard, and give me a sense of his nearness in such degree as Thy laws permit.

If in aught I can minister to his peace, be pleased of Thy love to let this be; and mercifully keep me from every act which may mar the fullness of our joy when the end of the days hath come.

Pardon, O gracious Lord and Father, whatever is amiss in this my prayer, for my will is blind and erring, but Thou canst do exceeding abundantly above all that we ask or think: through Jesus Christ our Lord.

Anon.

November 14

O GOD, to me who am left to mourn his departure, grant that I may not sorrow as one without hope for my beloved who sleeps in Thee; but that, always remembering his courage, and the love that united us on earth, I may begin again with new courage to serve Thee more fervently who art the only source of true love and true fortitude: that, when I have passed a few more days in this valley of tears and in this shadow of death, supported by Thy rod and staff, I may see him again face to face, in those pastures and beside those waters of comfort where I believe he already walks with Thee. O Shepherd of the sheep, have pity upon this darkened soul of mine.

ARCHBISHOP BENSON

November 15

UNTO Thy tender and searching compassion, O Lord, do we commit all those who have died with little faith and few good deeds; those who were blinded to Thy glory by our unfaithfulness; and all who have never known Thy gospel. Grant that these, when they awaken to Thy presence and see Thee as Thou art, may know the greatness of Thy mercy; through Jesus Christ our Lord.

New Every Morning

O Christ, a light transcendent
Shines in Thy countenance,
And none can tell the sweetness,
The beauty of Thy glance.

In this may Thy poor servants
Their joy eternal find;
Thou calledst them, O rest them,
Thou Lover of mankind.

ST. JOHN DAMASCENE

November 16

> O LORD,
> Who healest the broken-hearted
> And bindest up their wounds,
> Grant Thy consolation unto the mourners . . .
>
> O strengthen and support them
> In the day of their grief and sorrow;
> And remember them (and their children)
> For a long and good life.
>
> Put into their hearts the fear and love of Thee,
> That they may serve Thee with a perfect heart;
> And let their latter end be peace.
>
> *Jewish Prayer*
> *Authorized Daily Prayer Book*

November 17

ALMIGHTY God, Father of mercies and giver of all comfort; Deal graciously, we pray Thee, with all those who mourn, that, casting every care on Thee, they may know the consolation of Thy love; through Jesus Christ our Lord.

Book of Common Prayer, 1928

Have compassion, O most merciful Lord, on all who are mourning for those dear to them, and all who are lonely and desolate. Be Thou their Comforter and Friend; give them such earthly solace as Thou seest

to be best for them; and bringing them to the fuller
knowledge of Thy love, do Thou wipe away all their
tears; for the sake of Jesus Christ our Lord.

Anon.

November 18

THE gates of heaven mayest thou find opened,
And the tower of peace mayest thou see,
And the dwellings of confidence,
And angels of peace to meet thee with joy;
And may the High Priest stand to receive thee;
And thou,
Go thou to the end,
For thou shalt rest,
And rise up again . . .

The gates of the sanctuary may Michael open,
And bring the soul as an offering before God;
And may the redeeming angel accompany thee
Unto the gates of the Heavens, where Israel dwells;
May it be vouchsafed to thee
To stand in this beautiful place;
And thou,
Go thou to the end,
For thou shalt rest,
And rise up again.

Jewish Prayer
Sephardi Prayer Book

November 19

BRING us, O Lord, God, at the last awakening into the house and gate of heaven, to enter into that gate and dwell in that house, where there shall be no darkness nor dazzling, but one equal light; no noise nor silence, but one equal music; no fears nor hopes, but an equal possession; no ends nor beginnings, but one equal eternity; in the habitations of Thy majesty and Thy glory, world without end.

JOHN DONNE

November 20

ST. PAUL

FOR this cause I bow my knees unto the Father of our Lord Jesus Christ, of whom the whole family in heaven and earth is named, that He would grant you, according to the riches of His glory, to be strengthened with might by His Spirit in the inner man; that Christ may dwell in your hearts by faith; that ye, being rooted and grounded in love, may be able to comprehend with all saints what is the breadth, and length, and depth, and height; and to know the love of Christ, which passeth knowledge, that ye might be filled with all the fullness of God. Now unto him that is able to do exceeding abundantly above all that we ask or think, according to the power that worketh in us, unto Him be glory in the church by Christ Jesus throughout all ages, world without end. Amen.

November 21

ST. AUGUSTINE

O LORD, my God, Light of the blind and Strength of the weak; yea also, Light of those that see, and Strength of the strong; hearken unto my soul, and hear it crying from the depths.

O Lord, help us to turn and seek Thee; for Thou hast not forsaken Thy creatures as we have forsaken Thee, our Creator. Let us turn and seek Thee, for we know

Thou art here in our hearts, when we confess to Thee, when we cast ourselves upon Thee, and weep in Thy bosom, after all our rugged ways; and Thou dost gently wipe away our tears, and we weep the more for joy; because Thou, Lord, who madest us, dost remake and comfort us.

Hear, Lord, my prayer, and grant that I may most entirely love Thee, and do Thou rescue me, O Lord, from every temptation, even unto the end.

November 22

ST. THOMAS AQUINAS

GIVE me, O Lord, a steadfast heart, which no unworthy affection may drag downwards; give me an unconquered heart, which no tribulation can wear out; give me an upright heart, which no unworthy purpose may tempt aside. Bestow upon me also, O Lord my God, understanding to know Thee, diligence to seek Thee, wisdom to find Thee, and a faithfulness that may finally embrace Thee.

ST. JEROME

O good Shepherd, seek me out, and bring me home to Thy fold again. Deal favourably with me according to Thy good pleasure, till I may dwell in Thy house all the days of my life, and praise Thee for ever and ever with them that are there.

ST. FRANCIS OF ASSISI

LORD, make me an instrument of Thy peace.
Where there is hatred, let me sow love;
Where there is injury, pardon;
Where there is doubt, faith;
When there is despair, hope;
Where there is darkness, light;
When there is sadness, joy.

O Divine Master, grant that
I may not so much seek
To be consoled, as to console;
Not so much to be understood as
To understand; not so much to be
Loved as to love:
For it is in giving that we receive;
It is in pardoning, that we are pardoned;
It is in dying, that we awaken to eternal life.

ST. CATHERINE OF SIENA

THOU, Eternal Trinity, art a sea so deep that the more
I enter therein, the more I find; and the more I find, the
more I seek of Thee; for when the soul is satisfied in
Thine abyss, it is not satisfied, but it ever continues to
thirst for Thee, Eternal Trinity, desiring to behold Thee
with the light of Thy light. As the hart panteth after
the water brooks, so does my soul desire to issue from the

prison of the darksome body, and to behold Thee in truth. O how long shall Thy face be hidden from my eyes? O Abyss, O Eternal Godhead. O Deep Sea! Robe me with Thyself, Eternal Trinity, so that I may run this mortal life with true obedience, and with the light of Thy most holy faith.

November 25

ST. PATRICK'S BREASTPLATE

I BIND unto myself to-day
The power of God to hold and lead,
His eye to watch, His might to stay,
His ear to hearken to my need.
The wisdom of my God to teach,
His hand to guide, His shield to ward,
The word of God to give me speech,
His heavenly host to be my guard.

Christ be with me, Christ within me,
Christ behind me, Christ before me,
Christ beside me, Christ to win me,
Christ to comfort and restore me.
Christ beneath me, Christ above me,
Christ in quiet, Christ in danger,
Christ in hearts of all that love me,
Christ in mouth of friend and stranger.

ST. BASIL

O LORD our God, teach us, we beseech Thee, to ask Thee aright for the right blessings. Steer Thou the vessel of our life toward Thyself, Thou tranquil haven of all storm-tossed souls. Show us the course wherein we should go. Renew a willing spirit within us. Let Thy spirit curb our wayward senses, and guide and enable us unto that. which is our true good, to keep Thy laws, and in all our works evermore to rejoice in Thy glories and gladdening Presence. For Thine is the glory and praise from all Thy saints for ever and ever.

ST. JOHN OF DAMASCUS

From my lips in their defilement,
From my heart in its beguilement,
From my tongue which speaks not fair,
From my soul stained, everywhere,
O, my Jesus, take my prayer!

Spurn me not for all it says,
Not for words, and not for ways,
Not for shamelessness endured!
Make me brave to speak my mood,
O my Jesus, as I would!
Or teach me, which I rather seek,
What to do and what to speak.

November 28

ST. IGNATIUS OF LOYOLA

FILL us, we pray Thee, with Thy light and life, that we may show forth Thy wondrous glory. Grant that Thy love may so fill our lives that we may count nothing too small to do for Thee, nothing too much to give, and nothing too hard to bear. So teach us, Lord, to serve Thee as Thou deservest, to give and not to count the cost, to fight and not to heed the wounds, to toil and not to seek for rest, to labour and not to ask for any reward save that of knowing that we do Thy will.

November 29

ST. THOMAS MORE

ALMIGHTY God, have mercy on —— and —— and on all that bear me evil will, and would me harm, and their faults and mine together, by such easy, tender, merciful means as Thine infinite wisdom can divine, vouchsafe to amend and redress, and make us saved souls in heaven together where we may ever live and love together with Thee and Thy blessed saints, O glorious Trinity, for the bitter passion of our sweet Saviour Christ.

O LORD our God, grant us grace to desire Thee with our whole heart; that, so desiring, we may seek, and seeking find Thee; and so finding Thee may love Thee; and loving Thee, may hate those sins from which Thou hast redeemed.

November 30

ST. PHILIPPO DE NERI

O LORD, put no trust in me; for I shall surely fail if Thou uphold me not.

ST. CATHERINE OF GENOA

O Love, no more sins! no more sins!

ST. FRANÇOIS DE SALES

O all-good God, Thou dost not forsake unless forsaken, Thou never takest away Thy gifts until we take away our hearts.

ST. CLEMENT

O God, make us children of quietness, and heirs of peace.

Thankful in mind,
Thankful in heart,
Thankful in soul and body,
I worship Thee, O my God,
I magnify and glorify Thee,
Who art blessed both now
And for evermore.

DECEMBER

DEATH AND JUDGEMENT

FOR CHILDREN

CHRISTMAS

ALL after pleasure as I rid one day,
  My horse and I, both tired, body and mind,
With full cry of affections, quite astray,
  I took up in the next inn I could find.

There when I came, whom found I but my dear,
  My dearest Lord, expecting till the grief
Of pleasures brought me to Him, ready there
  To be all passengers' most sweet relief.

O Thou, whose glorious yet contracted light,
   Wrapt in Night's mantle, stole into a manger,
Since my dark soul and brutish, is Thy right,
   To man, of all beasts, be not Thou a stranger:

Furnish and deck my soul, that Thou mayest have
A better lodging than a rack or grave.

The shepherds sing; and shall I silent be?
   My God, no hymn for Thee?
My soul's a shepherd too; a flock it feeds
   Of thoughts and words and deeds:
The pasture is Thy word; the streams Thy grace,
   Enriching all the place.

Shepherd and flock shall sing, and all my powers
   Out-sing the daylight hours;
Then we will chide the Sun for letting Night
   Take up his place and right:
We sing one common Lord; wherefore He should
   Himself the candle hold.

I will go searching till I find a sun
   Shall stay till we have done;
A willing shiner, that shall shine as gladly
   As frost-nipped suns look sadly:
Then we will sing, and shine all our own day,
   And one another pay:

His beams shall cheer my breast, and both so twine,
Till ev'n His beams sing, and my music shine.

GEORGE HERBERT

Death and judgement

O LORD Jesus Christ, son of the living God, set Thine
holy Passion, Cross and Death between Thy judgement
and our souls, both now and in the hour of death. And
vouchsafe, we beseech Thee, to grant unto the living
mercy and grace, to the dead pardon and rest, to Thine
holy Church peace and concord, and to us miserable
sinners life and joy everlasting; who livest and reignest
with the Father and the Holy Ghost, one God, world
without end.

Primer of 1559

ALMIGHTY love! Where art thou now? Mad man
    Sits down, and freezeth on,
He raves, and swears to stir nor fire, nor fan,
    But bids the thread be spun.
I see, thy curtains are close-drawn; thy bow
    Looks dim too in the cloud,
Sin triumphs still, and man is sunk below
    The centre, and his shroud;
All's in deep sleep, and night; thick darkness lies
    And hatcheth o'er thy people;
But hark! What trumpet's that? What angel cries
    Arise! Thrust in thy sickle.

HENRY VAUGHAN

December 3

MAKE us, we beseech thee, O Lord our God, in watch-fulness and eagerness to look for the coming of Christ Thy Son our Lord; that when He shall come and knock, He may not find us sleeping in our sins, but watching and exulting in his praises.

Gelasian Sacramentary

Let me love Thee, O Christ,
in Thy first coming,
when Thou wast made man, for love of men,
and for love of me.

Let me love Thee, O Christ,
in Thy second coming,
when with an inconceivable love
Thou standest and knockest at the door,
and wouldest enter into the souls of men,
and into mine.

Plant in my soul, O Christ, Thy likeness of love;
that when by death Thou callest,
it may be ready,
and burning
to come unto Thee.

ERIC MILNER-WHITE
My God my Glory

. . . O, THAT Fire! before whose face
Heav'n and earth shall find no place:
O, those Eyes! whose angry light
Must be the day of that dread Night . . .

But Thou giv'st leave, dread Lord, that we
Take shelter from Thyself in Thee;
And with the wings of Thine own dove
Fly to the sceptre of soft love.

Dear, remember in that day
Who was the cause Thou cam'st this way:
Thy sheep was stray'd, and Thou wouldst be
Even lost Thyself in seeking me!

RICHARD CRASHAW
From *Dies Irae* in *Sacred Poems*

December 5

O LORD, raise up (we pray Thee) Thy power, and come among us, and with great might succour us; that whereas, through our sins, and wickedness, we are sore let and hindered in running the race that is set before us, Thy bountiful grace and mercy may speedily help and deliver us; through the satisfaction of Thy Son our Lord, to whom with Thee and the Holy Ghost be honour and glory, world without end.

Book of Common Prayer

December 6

O LORD Jesu, our only health and our everlasting life, I give myself wholly unto Thy will: being sure that the thing cannot perish which is committed unto Thy mercy.

Thou, merciful Lord, wast born for my sake: Thou didst suffer both hunger and thirst for my sake; Thou didst preach and teach, didst pray and fast, for my sake: and finally Thou gavest Thy most precious body to die and Thy blood to be shed on the cross, for my sake. Most merciful Saviour, let all these things profit me which Thou freely hast given me. O Lord, into Thy hands I commit my soul.

Primer of 1559
Repeated by Thomas Cromwell on the scaffold

December 7

THOU knowest, Lord, the secrets of our hearts; shut not Thy merciful ears to our prayer; but spare us, Lord most holy, O God most mighty, O holy and merciful Saviour. Thou most worthy Judge eternal, suffer us not, at our last hour, for any pains of death, to fall from Thee.

Anon.

A Christian close, without sin, without shame, and, should it please Thee, without pain, and a good answer at the dreadful and fearful judgement seat of Jesus Christ our Lord, vouchsafe, O Lord.

LANCELOT ANDREWES
The Private Prayers of Lancelot Andrewes

DEATH

CHRIST leads me through no darker rooms
Than He went through before;
He that unto God's kingdom comes,
Must enter by this door . . .

My knowledge of that life is small,
The eye of faith is dim;
But 'tis enough that Christ knows all,
And I shall be with him.

RICHARD BAXTER

December 9

O LORD, the First and the Last, the Beginning and the
End, who wast with us in our birth, be with us through
our life; Thou who art with us through our life, be with
us at our death; and because Thy mercy will not leave
us then, grant that we die not, but rise to the life everlasting with Thee and in Thee; who livest and reignest
in the glory of the eternal Trinity, one God, world
without end.

ERIC MILNER-WHITE
A Cambridge Bede Book

December 10

PRESERVE my soul, O Lord, because it belongs to Thee, and preserve my body because it belongs to my soul. Thou alone dost steer my boat through all its voyage, but hast a more especial care of it, when it comes to a narrow current, or to a dangerous fall of waters. Thou hast a care of the preservation of my body in all the ways of my life; but, in the straits of death, open Thine eyes wider, and enlarge Thy Providence towards me so far that no illness or agony may shake and benumb the soul. Do Thou so make my bed in all my sickness that, being used to Thy hand, I may be content with any bed of Thy making.

JOHN DONNE

December 11

MY Lord, give me to know Thee, to believe on Thee, to love Thee, to serve Thee, to live to and for Thee. Give me to die just at that time and in that way which is most for Thy glory.

CARDINAL NEWMAN

O blessed Jesu, most mighty lion, King immortal and most victorious, have mind of the sorrow that Thou sufferedst when all the powers of Thine heart and body for feebleness failed Thee utterly. And then Thou saidst, inclining Thine head thus: "It is all done." For mind of thine anguish and sorrow, blessed Jesus, have mercy on me in my last end.

Sarum Primer, 1538

December 12

LORD, I am coming as fast as I can. I know I must pass through the shadow of death, before I can come to Thee. But it is but *umbra mortis*, a mere shadow of death, a little darkness upon nature: but Thou, by Thy merits and passion, hast broken through the jaws of death. So, Lord, receive my soul, and have mercy upon me; and bless this kingdom with peace and plenty, and with brotherly love and charity, that there may not be this effusion of Christian blood amongst them, for Jesus Christ His sake, if it be Thy will.

ARCHBISHOP WILLIAM LAUD
When kneeling at the block

December 13

BEFORE the beginning Thou hast foreknown the end,
Before the birthday the death-bed was seen of Thee:
Cleanse what I cannot cleanse, mend what I cannot
    mend,
    O Lord All-Merciful, be merciful to me.

While the end is drawing near I know not mine end;
Birth I recall not, my death I cannot foresee:
O God, wise to defend, wise to befriend,
    O Lord All-Merciful, be merciful to me.

CHRISTINA ROSSETTI

For children

A BAPTISM BLESSING

Thou Being who inhabitest the heights
Imprint Thy blessing betimes,
Remember Thou the child of my body,
In Name of the Father of peace;
When the priest of the King
On him puts the water of meaning,
Grant him the blessing of the Three
   Who fill the heights
  The blessing of the Three
   Who fill the heights.

Sprinkle down upon him Thy grace,
Give Thou to him virtue and growth,
Give Thou to him strength and guidance,
Give Thou to him flocks and possessions,
Sense and reason void of guile,
Angel wisdom in his day,
That he may stand without reproach
   In Thy presence
  He may stand without reproach
   In Thy presence.

The Sun Dances
Prayers from the Gaelic

A BAPTISM PRAYER

ALMIGHTY and everlasting God, who by the Baptism of
Thy well-beloved Son Jesus Christ, in the river Jordan,
didst sanctify water to the mystical washing away of Sin;
Mercifully look upon this child; wash him and sanctify
him with the Holy Spirit, that he may be received into
the ark of Christ's Church; and being steadfast in faith,
joyful through hope, and rooted in charity, may so pass
the waves of this troublesome world, that finally he may
come to the land of everlasting life, there to reign with
Thee world without end; through Jesus Christ our Lord.

Book of Common Prayer, 1928

A MOTHER'S PRAYER

BESTOW Thy blessing upon Thy handmaid;
Strengthen and uphold me together with my husband,
That we may rear the child that has been born unto us
To fear Thee and to serve Thee in truth,
And to walk in the path of righteousness.
Keep the tender babe in all his ways.
Favour him with knowledge, and understanding and
    discernment,
And let his portion be in Thy Law,
So that he may sanctify Thy great name,
And become a comfort to us in our old age.

Jewish Prayer
Authorized Daily Prayer Book

December 17

FOR CHILDREN AND PARENTS

O LORD Jesus Christ, be near to all young children, that in the peril and confusion of this time their growing spirits may take no hurt at our hands; and grant to parents such sure knowledge of Thy love that they may guide their children with courage and with faith.

New Every Morning

Lord Jesus, who didst love little children and who taught us that of such is the kingdom of heaven, show us new ways of protecting them and a new determination to care for the children of all nations, that, growing up to know and love Thee, they may make the world more like Thy plan for it. So may Thy will be done on earth as it is in heaven.

LESLIE D. WEATHERHEAD
A Private House of Prayer

O LORD Jesus Christ, whose anger was once terribly kindled against those who hurt the children, we beseech you to bring to repentance all those who through cruelty, lust or carelessness bring the innocent to harm. We are among them, O Lord, and confess with sorrow and shame that every failure of our love in thought, word or deed immeasurably increases the sin of the world and the unhappiness of the children. Lord, have mercy on us, increase our love and consecrate it, making it active in deed and prayer for all children in danger of body, mind or spirit, all who are hungry or homeless through war or disaster, children of broken homes, frightened or lonely children, children who look for love and do not find it. What can we say, O Lord, what can we ask? They are the innocent sufferers for our sins, as you were in your life on earth, united to you more closely than we can understand. Lord, have mercy upon them in their suffering, and have mercy upon us in our sin.

LORD, as once the mothers of Israel brought their children to you that you might bless them, so now we come to you bringing with us in our hearts those children who are especially dear to each one of us. Kneeling in the shadow of your great love for them, your most glorious and perfect prayer to the Father for them, we say their names over in your presence . . . You alone know what awaits them in life, and the special needs of each one of them, and we humbly trust them to your never-failing

269

mercy and almighty love. We ask only that throughout their lives they may do and bear what is your will for them as perfectly as they are able, and that you will keep them close to you forever.

December 20

A CHILD'S PRAYER

LAMB of God, I look to thee;
Thou shalt my Example be;
Thou art gentle, meek and mild,
Thou wast once a little child.

Fain I would be as thou art;
Give me Thy obedient heart.
Thou art pitiful and kind;
Let me have Thy loving mind . . .

Thou didst live to God alone,
Thou didst never seek Thine own;
Thou Thyself didst never please.
God was all Thy happiness.

Loving Jesu, gentle Lamb,
In Thy gracious hands I am,
Make me, Saviour, what Thou art,
Live Thyself within my heart.

CHARLES WESLEY

Christmas

December 21

LORD, I will go to Mary and make covenant with her, to
keep her child, not for her need but for mine. And take
to me the sweet child and swathe Him in His cradle with
love bands. Lord, help me to put from me the cradle of
self love and draw to me the cradle of true love, for that
liketh this child to rest Him in, and so in my soul sing
lovelike and say:

> Lovely little child, fairest of hue,
> Have mercy on me, sweet Jesu.

And while I thus sing I will be sorry and think how oft
I have received my God and laid Him in a foul common
stable to all the seven deadly sins . . . and seldom fully
cleansed to God's liking; therefore oft sigh and sorrow
and shrive me to God as I rock the cradle, and sing and
say: Lovely little Child.

From *Book to a Mother*
Bodleian MS adapted

December 22

BLESSED be He Who cometh in the Name of the Lord,
and hath dawned upon us; Whose coming hath redeemed us, Whose nativity hath enlightened us; and
Who by His coming hath sought out the lost, and
illuminated those who sat in darkness. Grant, therefore,
O Father Almighty, that we, celebrating with pious
devotion the day of His nativity, may find the day of
judgement a day of mercy: that as we have known His
benignity as our Redeemer, we may feel his gentle tenderness as our Judge.

Mozarabic Liturgy

COME to me, Belovèd,
　Babe of Bethlehem;
Lay aside Thy sceptre
　And Thy diadem.

Come to me, Belovèd;
　Light and healing bring;
Hide my sin and sorrow
　Underneath Thy wing.

Bid all fear and doubting
　From my soul depart,
As I feel the beating
　Of Thy human heart . . .

Hide me from the pity
　Of the seraphin,
They, so pure and spotless,
　I, so stained with sin.

Hide me from St. Michael
　With his flaming sword—
Thou can'st understand me,
　O my human Lord! . . .

Only Thee, Belovèd,
　Only Thee, I seek.
Thou, the man Christ Jesus,
　Strength in flesh made weak.

D. M. DOLBEN

December 24: Christmas Eve

GOD, who has made this most holy night to shine with the brightness of the True Light, grant we beseech Thee that as on earth we have known the mystery of that Light, so also in heaven we may partake of its joys.

Gelasian Sacramentary

Come forth out of Thy royal chambers, O Prince of all the kings of the earth; put on the visible robes of Thy imperial majesty, take up that unlimited sceptre which Thy Almighty Father hath bequeathed Thee, for now the voice of Thy bride calls Thee, and all creatures sigh to be renewed.

JOHN MILTON

December 25: Christmas Day

MOONLESS darkness stands between,
Past, O Past, no more be seen!
But the Bethlehem star may lead me
To the sight of Him who freed me
From the self that I have been.
Make me pure, Lord: Thou art holy;
Make me meek, Lord: Thou wert lowly;
Now beginning, and alway:
Now begin, on Christmas day.

GERALD MANLEY HOPKINS

December 26

WELCOME, all wonders in one sight!
   Eternity shut in a span.
Summer in winter. Day in night.
   Heaven in earth, and God in man.
Great little one! whose all-embracing birth
Lifts earth to heaven, stoops heav'n to earth . . .

To Thee, meek majesty! soft king
   Of simple graces and sweet loves,
Each of us his lamb will bring
   Each his pair of silver doves;
Till burnt at last in fire of Thy fair eyes,
Our selves become our own best sacrifice.

RICHARD CRASHAW

December 27

WE beseech thee, O gracious Lord, let our hearts be enlightened by the holy radiance of Thy Son's Incarnation; that so we may escape the darkness of this world, and by His guidance attain to the country of everlasting clearness.

Sarum Missal

God, who makest us glad with the yearly remembrance of the birth of Thy only Son Jesus Christ; Grant that as we joyfully receive Him as our Redeemer, so we may with sure confidence behold Him, when He shall come to be our Judge, who liveth and reigneth with Thee and the Holy Ghost, now and forever.

Prayer Book, 1549

LORD when the wise men came from far
Led to Thy cradle by a star,
Then did the shepherds too rejoice,
Instructed by Thy angel's voice,
Blest were the wise men in their skill,
And shepherds in their harmless will . . .

There is no merit in the wise
But love, (the shepherds' sacrifice).
Wise men, all ways of knowledge past
To th' shepherds' wonder come at last;
To know, can only wonder breed,
And not to know, is wonder's seed.

SYDNEY GODOLPHIN

O LORD Christ Jesus, God that art ever saving men, and Man that alone hast power in God, we call upon Thee, we praise Thee, we beseech Thee be with us to spare, to pity, to forgive. Put in our hearts prayers that Thou mayest fulfil, put in our mouths words to which Thou mayest hearken, make us to do works that Thou mayest bless. Let faith that doubts not conceive Thee. Let mind set free from corruption give birth to Thee. Depart not from us, but come forth within us. Be Thou in truth our Emmanuel, God with us.

Mozarabic Missal
adapted

December 30

LORD God, who art the same yesterday, today, and for ever, whose throne is established in righteousness, whose compassions fail not, and whose love endureth unto all generations: Lift the light of Thy countenance upon us, pilgrims as all our fathers were, that thanking Thee for all the way by which Thou hast led us, we may as Thy children set our faces towards eternity and our affections on things above, ere we pass hence and are no more seen; through Jesus Christ our Lord.

B. J. SNELL
School Worship

December 31

> Now thank we all our God,
>   With heart and hands and voices,
>   Who wondrous things hath done,
> In whom His world rejoices;
>   Who from our mother's arms
>   Hath blessed us on our way
>   With countless gifts of love,
>   And still is ours to-day.
>
> O may this bounteous God
> Through all our life be near us,
>   With ever joyful hearts
> And blessed peace to cheer us;
>   And keep us in His grace,
>   And guide us when perplexed,
>   And free us from all ills
>   In this world and the next.

All praise and thanks to God
The Father now be given,
    The Son, and Him who reigns
With them in highest heaven,
    The One eternal God
        Whom earth and heaven adore;
For thus it was, is now,
        And shall be evermore. Amen.

M. RINKART
17th century

TRANSLATIONS AND MODERN EDITIONS

Prayers from the Ark by Carmen Bernos de Gasztold. Translated by Rumer Godden (Macmillan).

The Sun Dances. Translated from the Gaelic by Alexander Carmichael (Christian Community Press).

The Confessions of Saint Augustine. Translated by F. J. Sheed (Sheed & Ward).

The True Prayers of St. Gertrude and St. Mechtilde. Translated by Canon John Gray (Sheed & Ward).

The Private Prayers of Lancelot Andrewes. Edited by Hugh Martin (S.C.M. Press).

Visions from Piers Plowman. Translated by Nevill Coghill (Phoenix House Publications).

The Jewish Authorized Daily Prayer Book. Translated by the Rev. S. Singer (Eyre & Spottiswoode).

The Sephardi Prayer Book. Translated by D. A. de Sola (Oxford University Press).

The prayers of Jacopone da Todi. From the translation by Mrs. Theodore Beck, found in *Jacopone da Todi* by Evelyn Underhill (J. M. Dent).

Prayers from ancient MSS (pp. 57, 91, 138, 271). Found in *The Coasts of the Country*, edited by Clare Kirchberger (Harvill Press).

Poem by Paul Verlaine (p. 30). Translated by Arthur Symons (Source unidentified).

11th-century Jewish hymn (p. 34). Translated by Israel Zangwill (Source unidentified).

Prayer of John of Bonella (p. 48). From a booklet at the end of *The Spiritual Combat* (Longmans, Green).

Poem of Theodulf (p. 56). Translated by Helen Waddell and found in one of her lectures.

Poem of David of Gwylym (p. 78). Rendered by James Clarence Morgan (*Poems*, 1903).

Poem by Marcos Ana (p. 99). Translated by Chloe Vulliamy and Stephen Sedley and found in *From Burgos Jail*.

Caedmon's Hymn (p. 193). Translated by Kevin Crossley Holland in *The Battle of Maldon* edited by Bruce Mitchell (Macmillan).

A Saint (p. 235). Translated from Old High German by William Taylor (Source unidentified).

The prayer of Jeremy Taylor on p. 71; adaptation from Ecclesiasticus (p. 107); the prayer of Erasmus on p. 135; adaptation from Greek Vespers (p. 165); were found in *Daily Prayer* edited by Eric Milner-White and G. W. Briggs (Oxford University Press).

ACKNOWLEDGEMENTS

THE compiler and the publishers are grateful to the following for permission to include prayers in this anthology:

Geoffrey Bles Ltd. for extracts from C. S. Lewis's *Poems*.

The British Broadcasting Corporation for prayers taken from *New Every Morning*.

William Collins and Sons and Editions du Seuil, Paris, for the extract from Le Milieu Divin by Teilhard de Chardin.

Darton, Longman and Todd Ltd. for the prayer by Père Olier taken from *A Cowley Father's Letters*.

J. M. Dent and Sons Ltd. for the prayers taken from *Jacopone da Todi* by Evelyn Underhill; and for the extract from Nevill Coghill's translation of *Visions from Piers Plowman*.

The Epworth Press for the prayer from the *Methodist Shorter Book of Offices*.

The Harvill Press Ltd. for extracts from the anthology by Clare Kirchberger *The Coasts of the Country*.

William Heffer & Sons Ltd. for the poem of J. S. Hoyland.

The Houghton Mifflin Company (Boston, Mass.) for the poem of William Dean Howells.

Alfred A. Knopf Inc. (New York) for two extracts from *The Prophet* by Kahlil Gibran.

Longmans, Green & Co. Ltd. for extracts from *A Cambridge Bede Book* by Eric Milner-White.

Macmillan & Co. Ltd. and the Macmillan Company of Canada Ltd. for extracts from *Prayers from the Ark* by Carmen Bernos de Gasztold, translated by Rumer Godden; and for *Student Taper* from the Collected Poems of James Stephens; the latter also by permission of Mrs. Iris Wise.

A. R. Mowbray & Co. Ltd. for the prayer from the *Life and Letters of Father Andrew*; for extracts from *The Face of Love* by Gilbert Shaw; for prayers from *Memorials Upon Several Occasions* (published under the present title *After the Third Collect*).

The Oxford University Press for the poems of Gerard Manley Hopkins; for extracts from *A Diary of Private Prayer* by John

Baillie; for the poem of D. M. Dolben; for extracts from *Daily Prayer* by Eric Milner-White and G. W. Briggs; for the prayer by W. E. Orchard from the Order of Divine Service for Public Worship; for the hymn "Father most holy" translated by Percy Dearmer and found in *The English Hymnal*.

Routledge and Kegan Paul Ltd. for prayers from the Service of the Orthodox Synagogue.

St. Martin's Press Inc., The Macmillan Company of Canada and Macmillan & Co. Ltd., London, for the extract from *The Battle of Maldon* translated by Kevin Crossley-Holland and edited by Bruce Mitchell.

The S.C.M. Press Ltd. for prayers from *A Book of Prayers for Students*; and from *Jewish Prayer and Worship*.

Sheed & Ward Ltd. for extracts from the translation by F. J. Sheed of the *Confessions of St. Augustine*; and for the poem from *The Flowering Tree* by Caryll Houselander.

The Society for Promoting Christian Knowledge for prayers from *My God My Glory* by Eric Milner-White; and from *A Procession of Passion Prayers* also by Eric Milner-White.

The Trustees of the Tagore Estate and Macmillan & Co. Ltd. for the lines from *Gitanjali No X*, taken from the *Collected Poems and Plays of Rabindranath Tagore*.

The Literary Trustees of Walter de la Mare and The Society of Authors as their representative for the poem of Walter de la Mare.

The Father Provincial of the English Province of the Order of Preachers for extracts from *The True Prayers of St. Gertrude and St. Mechtilde*.

The Committee of the Appeal for Amnesty in Spain for the poem "Nightwatch" by Marcos Ana.

Miss Norah Thompson for her *Litany for the Animals*.

The Rt. Rev. Trevor Huddleston, C.R., for his prayer, *God Bless Africa*.

The Rt. Rev. Joost de Blank for his prayer for racial peace.

The Rev. Dr. Leslie D. Weatherhead, C.B.E., for two prayers

281

INDEX OF SOURCES